THE RENEGADE WRITER

A Totally Unconventional Guide
to Freelance Writing Success

3rd EDITION
REVISED & UPDATED

Linda Formichelli
Diana Burrell

Praise for
The Renegade Writer

"Round up all those so-called 'rules' you internalized about the Right Way to be a Freelancer and give them a good swift kick in the pants. Freelancers of all experience levels will benefit from the spirited and practical recommendations these two real-world freelancers offer. Perhaps the most striking feature of *The Renegade Writer* is its sheer readability. You can't help but devour the whole thing in one or two gluttonous sittings."

The Writer

"Full of great tips and common sense, the book demystifies all the stages of getting a piece published. Upbeat and exceptionally informative, this book is an excellent choice for both working and would-be writers."

Publishers Weekly

TABLE OF CONTENTS

A Free Gift for Our Readers!

We're offering a free gift to our readers:
a copy of our 1,400-page e-book
The Renegade Writer OMNIBUS:
Best of the Renegade Writer Blog 2006-2016.
Be sure to check out the offer at the end of this book!

Introduction

When did your writing dream start...and what happened to it?

Chances are, you were praised sometime early in your life for your writing efforts, but you buried that talent at law school, an advertising agency, a career in retail, or while raising your children. Yet every time you pick up an issue of *Redbook* or *National Geographic Traveler* or even *Pizza Today*, a prick of jealousy stabs you as you skim the bylines of writers who get paid to write about scientific advances in male arousal drugs or restaurants in Venice or the hottest new pizza toppings. And they do all this from a home office no less, while you have to suffer annoying co-workers and cranky clients from your corporate cubicle. You're making a living, but is it the living you dreamed of back in junior high?

Or perhaps you've already shucked the corporate chains for a life of freelance writing. You're emailing editors with earnest, typo-free story pitches, but your inbox (and checking account) is a little less full than you would like. Or maybe you've been plugging along for a couple of years, making a decent amount of money, but feel you still haven't realized your initial inspiration: You can't crack a dream magazine, or you feel like you've been pegged as a technology writer when you'd rather write about fine dining or human relationships.

Your lack of assignments could be because you're following all the rules.

Whether you're a seasoned freelancer or a wannabe writer, it's easy to believe the rumors, myths, and misconceptions about freelance writing. These bugaboos abound because freelancers work largely on their own, isolated from other writers, so they have no real-life examples to learn from. Sure, you probably belong to a dozen or so freelance discussion boards and Facebook groups, but those are full of writers offering advice using a sample size of one, with dubious qualifications backing it up.

But if you were to share office space with a group of professional magazine writers and observe them for weeks on end à la Jane Goodall, we guarantee that they'd shatter most every myth about freelancing you carry around in that fertile imagination of yours. Moreover, the world has changed, but the good people writing books on how to freelance seem not to have noticed this; some still urge writers to keep pitches to exactly one page, or advise writers to cop a servile attitude around editors.

Don't get us wrong—we adore all the books about writing on our office shelves. The two of us probably own enough of these tomes to span the distance between our houses and have studied a few of them better than any book we studied in college. The funny thing is, though, we've found that the rules in these books don't bring us the fame, the fortune, or at least the 1099s that we so desire.

And yet, here we are, asking you to read *our* writing book and bow in obeisance to our astute observations—are we shameless hypocrites or what? Please listen to our stories before you start gathering up stones to hurl.

Diana's Story

I didn't set out to be a magazine writer. No, for most of my life, my writerly goal was loftier: I wanted to be a novelist. I wanted to be a female J. D. Salinger, a chronicler of youthful angst, but Douglas Coupland beat me to it. Then I toyed with short fiction, and actually had a story published in my college's literary magazine. But short fiction won't get you rich, and soon my aspirations for fame had transformed into a yearning for A) a satisfying career that would B) meet or exceed my current standard of living.

With my expensive bachelor's degree in the liberal arts relegated to a back drawer, I spent 10 years in product marketing and advertising for several companies. I went through staff downsizings, computer upgrades, and mid-year reviews with bosses straight out of a Dilbert comic strip, during which my natural sense of curiosity about the world nearly shriveled up and died. Yes, I was making good money and traveling to places like Fayetteville, Arkansas, where I got to tour a chicken processing plant (also known as a slaughterhouse), but I didn't even have time to eat right or exercise, never mind write. When I found time to mull over the path my life had taken, I wondered what had happened to the girl whose goal in life was to be a writer.

A former boyfriend and I used to visit friends of his who had a summer place in the Hamptons, and as the fates would have it, one of them was a senior editor at a women's magazine in New York. One day while lounging poolside, I asked her about her job, and specifically about writing. Her informal comments gave me a crash course in the difference between a great freelancer and an editor's nightmare. She confirmed, for example, that most of the proposals landing on her desk were either not targeted to her magazine or poorly written. And the stuff that set the pros apart—taking criticism well, making deadlines, being pleasant to deal with—were things I knew I could do well, thanks to my corporate training. By the end of the conversation, the wheels were grinding in my head. Based on what she'd said, I knew freelance writing was a career in which I could succeed, even thrive.

I wish I could report that I marched back to my product marketing job in Connecticut, quit, and landed big assignments from major magazines. But no, I made the mistake a lot of beginning freelancers and wannabes make—I denied the siren's song. I changed jobs, hoping that I'd finally find fulfillment in another cubicle. (Nope. Nope. And nope. That's how many times I switched jobs before summoning the courage to go freelance.) I even thought about entering a full-time graduate program in English literature hoping that it would somehow propel me closer to my goal of writing for a living.

The only things that did pan out were classes in magazine writing and editing, but not for the reasons you might suspect. In one of them, I happened to befriend a classmate who was an assistant editor at the glossy, upscale *Connecticut Magazine*, which published features about interesting people, events, and places in the Nutmeg State. Around that time, I started writing a romance novel and attending local Romance Writers of America meetings. The women who attended these meetings, both published authors and wannabes, were a quirky, interesting bunch—perfect candidates for a profile. So I asked my new friend if I could send her a proposal, she said okay, and I fired off two single-spaced pages packed full of juicy details that I knew she couldn't resist. This was back in the day when you mailed pitches to editors. I was so confident she'd buy the idea, I even told the romance writers that the assignment was in the bag. (I considered this a positive mental attitude, not lying.)

Lucky for me, the assignment came through, so I didn't have to skulk back to the romance writers with my broken attitude. The writing and editing process with the magazine went well and as I worked on the assignment, I found myself yearning to work like this full time. Still, I hung back from sending out more proposals and continued to toil away in my latest marketing management job, complete with a psychopath boss and cutthroat cube jockeys.

The New York magazine editor may have planted the freelancing seed in my head, but my husband gets full credit for kindling the fire under my butt. Before we married, he convinced me to quit my job, move in with him up in Boston, and use some of my savings to jumpstart my new career. Like a doofus, I diddled the opportunity away, taking full-time jobs when money got uncomfortably low—but I did flex my freelancing muscles more and more: I became a freelance features correspondent for a chain of local newspapers and I sold my first article to a national consumer magazine, *Walking*.

I made the final leap right before our wedding. You see, I was working in a huge multinational company as a tech writer for a incompetent supervisor who could not write. Seriously. She was exceptionally talented at taking her frustrations out on those who *could* write. One day she publicly berated me for looking off into space. (I was *thinking*, an activity that was somewhat alien to her.) When I called my fiancé at lunchtime and told him what happened, he said, "If you don't quit today, I will come over there and quit for you." Now, my husband is one of those guys who says what he means and means what he says; he wasn't kidding. I could hear the car keys jingling in his hand. And that's when it finally hit me: I was tired of not being happy with the work I was doing. I went back to my office, wrote up a resignation letter, walked into the dimwit's office and gave her my two weeks. Obviously, knowing that my husband-to-be was going to be my sugar daddy while I built my writing career made quitting a bit easier—and certainly less stressful.

There's an old saying, "A bad day fishing beats a good day at work." That's how I feel about freelancing: rejection letters, rewrites, slow payments...I wouldn't trade them for anything except for more acceptances, no rewrites, and direct deposit. We've got solid health insurance, saved for retirement, bought a house, and taken excellent vacations, so I don't buy the whole "starving freelancer" myth. And before you assume my husband has a high-flying corporate job to back me up, for years he was an independent consultant, as reliant upon the market and self-motivation as any freelance writer.

Even when the publishing world is in flux, I'm happier than ever to have the job I have. Sure, some of my best print markets have disappeared in the past few years, but I jumped on board with blogging, teaching, and self-publishing, which give me even more control over my income as I'm not reliant on traditional publishing anymore. Best of all, the flexibility of freelancing gave me the gift of being able to stay home with our son, who is now in high school, while earning income that kept our family afloat during some tough times. In the years since we wrote the first edition of *The Renegade Writer*, I've been offered several corporate jobs, one of which happened to be my dream job at my dream publication. I turned them all down. To paraphrase Michael Kors, freelancing isn't for sissies, but for flexibility, self-autonomy, and the pleasure of indulging a mile-wide curiosity streak, it can't be beat.

Linda's Story

I always wanted to be a writer, and like Diana, I dreamed of setting the world on fire with my fiction. In high school, I wrote all sorts of teenage-angsty stories and poems, two of which were printed in the high school literary magazine: A poem about a girl who was so smart that her head exploded, and a short story about a psychology student who suffered from various mental illnesses as he wrote about them on his final exam.

In college, my love of language headed for fresh borders and I left English behind to major in Russian and minor in German, hoping to become a translator. I ended up with a master's degree in Slavic linguistics—and a student loan debt that had me fearing time in Siberia to work it off. In the meantime, the creative writing had fallen by the wayside.

After grad school, I got it into my head to go into publishing, so I went on informational interviews at several publishing companies. I didn't like what I learned about the business, but I thought the experience would make a great article. I read *Queries and Submissions* by Thomas Clark, wrote up my first query, bought a copy of *Writer's Market*, picked out a few career magazines, and sent the queries off to the pubs. (Simultaneous submissions *and* pitching magazines I wasn't familiar with—see, I'm a rule-breaker from way back!)

Several weeks later, I had an assignment from *EEO Bimonthly* magazine—for $500! I almost cried with delight. After that, I sold a similar article to an online magazine called *Edge*. The editor was so pleased with my work that he passed my name along to the magazine's sister publications. From that recommendation I ended up with supremely unglamorous—yet dollar-producing—assignments from *AKFCF Quarterly*, the magazine for KFC franchisees, and *QSR Success*, a magazine for the quick service restaurant industry (what you and I call "fast food joints").

Things took off from there, and soon I was writing part-time from the apartment I shared with my husband while working at an office job three days per week.

When my husband transferred to a college near Boston in mid-1997, I decided to make the jump to full-time freelancing. We saved up enough money to squeak by for three months, with the understanding that if I didn't turn a profit by the end of that time, I would have to hit the want ads for a full-time position.

But turn a profit I did, and by working hard for trade magazines and smaller newsstand pubs, as well as for copywriting clients, I earned enough to support my husband and myself while he finished his degree.

Two years later, I was still loving the freelance lifestyle, but frustrated that I hadn't been able to break into any of the larger newsstand magazines. Dozens of pitches boomeranged with form rejections. But perseverance paid off, and one day I received a call from an editor at *Woman's Day* saying that she liked my idea—how to save money on big-ticket items like appliances and furniture—but that she preferred to see longer, better-researched queries. And here I had been following the one-page query rule like a good little writer! So I started writing two- and three-page queries, and that fall I landed lucrative assignments from *Woman's Day*, *Redbook*, and *Family Circle*. I had made it!

When my husband Eric graduated from college, he decided to go freelance with me. Since I was trying to move up in the writing world, when my trade editors called with assignments, I told them that I could no longer work for 20 cents per word, but that my husband would be happy to give it a go. The hand-off worked, and Eric and I started writing for many of the same magazines.

At the same time, I dropped much of the copywriting work I had been doing to concentrate on magazines. Since I started landing better-paying assignments, I was able to cut my work schedule down to around 20 hours per week and still pay the bills. I started offering an e-course on magazine writing in 2006, and in 2013, teamed up with Carol Tice, owner of the Freelance Writers Den, to create UsefulWritingCourses.com, where we developed even more classes for freelance writers—including some where we hired editors from well-known magazines to critique students' work. That's right, the editors were now on *our* payroll! Eric freelanced for magazines until 2011 and was then hired as the News Editor at BoardGameGeek.com; he still writes from home.

The writing life has been good to us. I was able to support the both of us while Eric completed his college degree, and we bought our first house in 2000. We're now living in our third house, in North Carolina. We were able to adopt a child, and we've traveled the world with him, from New York and Paris to Tokyo and Beijing. We have health insurance, we have retirement accounts, and we go on vacation every year. We also have plenty of time for hobbies and entertaining.

I achieved this success only by breaking the rules of freelancing that writing magazines and books had tried to impose on me—rules that sound good to a beginner or novice but that in practice only served to trip me up.

After years spent separating the phony from the bologna, I've learned that each writer needs to create their own rules.

Why We Wrote This Book

In August 2000, Linda was lunching at a Thai restaurant in Boston with her editor at *1099*, an online publication for freelancers. The conversation was all about writing, as it often is when writers gather, and Linda insisted that the one-page query letter rule was stupid; in fact, she said, she had better luck selling articles with three-page queries. "I should write an article on writing rules that should be broken," she huffed.

"Forget the article," this editor said. "That would make a great book."

The proverbial light bulb went on in her head. A book!

When Linda told her about the concept, Diana immediately got it. Although Diana had pored over books on freelance writing and listened to advice from more experienced journalists, she'd discovered along the way that she had more success when she followed her instincts or did the opposite of what everyone else was doing. Linda pulled a proposal together, and she and Diana wrote up three sample chapters.

Over the course of a year, Linda sent the proposal to 15 publishers. Each time, her self-addressed envelope came back fat with rejection (if it came back at all).

She also looked into teaming up with a well-known author who had a franchise of business books. Here's the deal he offered: Diana and Linda would do all the writing, editing, and promotion; the famous author's name would be listed first on the cover; and the famous author would pocket 50 percent of the royalties. Diana and Linda's counteroffer: Get bent.

Fast forward to September 2002, more than two years after Linda had written the proposal. Out of nowhere, she received an email from an editor she had written for at a printing industry trade magazine in the late 1990s when she was starting out.

"I now run a publishing company that publishes books for writers," he wrote. "Do you have any ideas for me?"

Did Linda have any ideas?! After wiping the tea from her monitor, she replied, "Why, yes, I so happen to have a full-fledged proposal for a book about freelance writing languishing on my hard drive." After calling Diana to tell her the news, Linda put together the proposal and sample chapters and emailed them to the publisher.

Within a week we had a deal. The three of us hashed out the details of the contract, and it was settled. We were going to write a book!

The Renegade Writer hit a nerve with readers. Writers loved it, and it became their freelancing bible. We were invited to conferences and writers' groups to talk about everything from idea generation to story research. In 2006 we released a second edition, and wrote a follow-up title, *The Renegade Writer's Query Letters That Rock*.

Soon after this, our dear publisher Ed decided to sell his company, and that's when our fortunes took a bad turn. The new owners talked a good game, but didn't seem to have a clue about running a publishing company. Even worse, though our books were selling well, the new owners weren't paying us the royalties they owed us.

We asked a lawyer to look at our contract, and she pointed out that our publisher had voided the contract by not paying our royalties. We sent them a legal letter, and soon we had the publishing rights to our two books back in our hands. So what did we do? We did the renegade thing and started our own publishing company, Renegade Writer Press! Thanks to platforms like Amazon.com's Kindle Direct Publishing, Createspace, and Barnes & Noble's Nook Press, along with the availability of independent book cover designers, editors, proofreaders, and marketing geniuses, it's easier than ever for smart authors to control the whole process of book publishing—and make more money in most cases.

As you flip through the chapters of our book, you'll see that each subhead invites you to "break this rule." We included rules that we've read in books and magazines, or that we've heard on the street (and online) from our peers. We also talked to a lot of writers who generously shared their rules—and rule-breaking experiences—with us.

Many of these rules are serviceable, but need a tune-up. Other rules are simply outdated. For example, editors drum into our heads to read back issues of their magazines, but with the publishing industry in such flux, sometimes you're better off following other strategies to understand their editorial direction. You'll note that the rules sometimes even contradict one another—for example, "Consider public relations people your friends," and "Treat PR people as enemies."

In the ten years that have passed since the second edition of this book was published, we've discovered even more rules to break, so you'll find plenty of new material and inspiration for your career within. We've checked in with the writers we interviewed for the second edition so we could update you on their lives and how their writing careers have evolved and changed, as well as added stories from a few new "renegades."

We advise you to skim the book and look for the rules that you've been following in your career, then read what we have to say about them. You may find that a small adjustment in your marketing strategy or writing process can make a big difference in your bottom line. If you're still drumming up the courage to make the jump into freelancing, the chapter "Starting Out" is for you. If you've been submitting pitches to one market at a time but are experiencing so-so results, you definitely need to read our chapter on "No-Fear Marketing." And even if you're doing great, you can still boost your productivity and income by taking a closer look at the "rules" you've been working under.

CHAPTER 1

Breaking In by Breaking Rules: Even New Freelancers Can Be Renegades

Misconceptions about getting started often hold new writers back. You may think that to be successful as a freelance writer, you need a J-school degree, an impressive database of editorial contacts, and a truckload of supplies. None of this matters. Read on to find out how you can get started now—even if your home office consists of the kitchen table and your most impressive "contact" is your high school English teacher.

Start at the bottom.

This self-imposed roadblock is one we hear all the time: New writers have to start in the Little Leagues before angling for the Majors. We know one self-proclaimed publishing expert who tells parenting writers they need to sell fifteen articles to regional parenting publications before they can pitch to national parenting publications. We call B.S.

Plenty of writers began at the top, such as writing superstar Kelly James; her first article assignment was from *Cosmopolitan*! And Diana's first assignment was from *Connecticut Magazine*—not exactly a brand-name title, but one that's read by her friends and family throughout her home state.

It probably sounds reasonable and less scary to approach a smaller, less visible publication if you're still wet behind the ears. You might believe that a rejection from *The Podunk Times* smarts less than one from *The New York Times*. Or you may have heard that smaller publications are eager to work with writers who lack many (or any) writing credits.

While there's truth in that second statement, if you're a new freelancer with confidence in your skills and compelling, salable ideas in your back pocket, why not skip the low-paying pubs and aim for the top of the heap? When Diana started writing full time, she spent way too much time pitching smaller publications. She figured getting work from the smaller publications would be easy, but she found that smaller pubs naturally had smaller staffs and budgets, so they were very unresponsive or would offer insultingly low pay.

Once, Diana had a terrific idea that she pitched to local newspapers, which never responded. Then she realized the story was perfect for *The New York Times*. She fired off a pitch to the editor who handled the section that she wanted to write for, and within an hour, he wrote back, advising her to contact another staff editor about the idea. She did, and the next morning the second editor wrote back, declining the idea since they'd done something similar a few months back, but inviting her to send more ideas. This was enough for Diana to realize that she'd rather get a friendly rejection from the Gray Lady than the cold shoulder from the 2-cents-per-word local rags stacked for free in her neighborhood grocery store.

Now before you come after us with a tire iron for insulting small publications, we do know that plenty of low-paying, small-staff publications employ appreciative, bright editors who treat copy with respect. We even write for a few of these publications because their PITA (Pain In The A**) rating is low. But don't let stupid rules like "You have to pay your dues" or "You have to sell to 15 regional parenting publications before pitching at the national level" prevent you from pitching *The Wall Street Journal* or *Smithsonian* or any other top-name publication.

Of course, you probably don't want to put all your eggs in one basket by pitching only the big guys, but don't be afraid to take a crack at them, even if you're a beginner. If you're already a good writer, you have nothing to lose and everything to gain. And if the biggies don't bite, you always have the smaller guys as a backup.

BREAK THIS RULE

Prepare to be poor.

New writers usually enter the field expecting to scrape by in service to their art. Writing is so interesting and fun, no one would ever pay good money for it! This "rule" is perpetuated by content mills (more on those later) and other bottom-feeder businesses that stand to benefit from your maintaining the poverty mindset.

One of the most popular blog posts Linda ever wrote, with over 7,000 shares, was a piece for Copyblogger on how to earn $250 per hour as a freelance writer. She was uniquely suited to write this post because, well, that's her normal hourly rate for the writing she does, whether it's magazine journalism, content writing, or copywriting. In the post she offered up her tips on how to command premium prices, but probably the most helpful thing for her readers was experiencing the mind-shift that writing is a valuable service that many people, publications, and businesses need and are willing to pay top dollar to obtain.

Of course, some writers couldn't wrap their heads around this; in fact, one writer went so far as to troll the reviews of one of her and Diana's books on Amazon, calling Linda a charlatan because it's simply not possible to earn that much writing.

Except that it is, and many writers earn this much (and more) because they know the true value of their offerings. As Tara Gentile writes in her book *The Art of Earning*, "Just because something is easy for you doesn't mean it's not valuable for your customers. [...] What is easy to you, what comes naturally and beautifully to you, is ugly, difficult, and downright nasty to someone else."

Writing may be your passion, but not many others have the ability to write in a way that educates and persuades...a way that helps clients garner more readers, boost loyalty, and earn profits. If you can do that, you're worth a good deal more than you probably think, and you'll find clients who feel the same way.

BREAK THIS RULE

You need to attend journalism school, or at least have a degree in English.

If that were so, magazines would sure be a lot skinnier. Freelance writers come from all backgrounds, and those backgrounds often don't include degrees in English or journalism. Linda studied Slavic linguistics in graduate school. Her husband Eric, who was also a freelancer for over a decade, has a degree in math. And while Diana minored in English as an undergraduate, her ten years in product marketing are what gave her the freelancing skills she needed to make it on the outside. Another freelancer we know, Kelly James, "escaped" from the law—that is, she trained as an attorney, but gave up litigation in 1997 to become a successful health and fitness writer. We know other writers who worked as nurses, teachers, and nonprofit administrators prior to freelancing.

In fact, an educational or career background in something other than journalism or English literature can give you a huge advantage as a freelancer. You're a CPA? Great! You'll have a leg up when pitching a story to *Cosmopolitan* on how smart gals can save for a rainy day. (Not to mention you'll be way ahead of other freelancers come April 15.) You practice medicine? There's a real need for writers with strong medical backgrounds to write health articles. A stay-at-home mom or dad with three children? Boy, what parenting publication editors would give to pick your brain for a day. You probably carry enough raw material in there to pay for advanced degrees for all of your kids.

But what if you don't have a degree, or you dropped out of college your junior year? It's still not an impediment to a successful career as a freelancer. (Check out our profile of über-successful writer Carol Tice.) No editor is ever going to conditionally accept one of your story ideas until you provide him with college transcripts—or even ask where you were educated. Editors really don't care, except maybe if you meet them at a social event and it comes up in small talk, and even then, it's a curiosity thing, not an assignment requirement. You may find you get more admiration and respect from your editors for being good at your job when the only degree you have is from the school of hard knocks.

Do keep in mind, however, that successful writers with interesting backgrounds and/or minimal formal education have a solid grasp of spelling, grammar, and the mind-boggling complexities of the English language. Nothing—and we mean nothing—annoys editors more than receiving emails filled with sorry spelling, ghastly grammar, and pitiful punctuation. We guarantee that if you commit these blunders, you won't have to worry about writing the article.

If you suspect your writing is a prime candidate for the recycling bin, find someone who will be your informal editor before you send stuff out. Pay this saintly person if you have to, in cash or chocolate. Notice which mistakes you make over and over again, and learn how to fix them yourself. Bookmark a few grammar sites (*The Elements of Style* is available online for free) and a dictionary site, and when in doubt, look it up!

You can't focus on your writing career when you have young children.

One of the most amazing truths Diana found out after having her son was that becoming a parent made her a more efficient—thus more productive—writer. When she didn't have children, she felt free to take her time pitching or to procrastinate by surfing the web. Then, when Diana came back from her maternity leave, she hired a babysitter to watch her son for fifteen hours a week. Those fifteen hours were the only time she had to finish her work, and finish her work she did. (Besides, she had to earn the money to pay the babysitter. That was motivating in itself.) By the end of the summer, Diana found she'd earned more that summer than she had in a whole year!

Shortly after Diana went back to writing full time, she and her husband decided to host an au pair from Germany to help with childcare. Melanie watched their son forty hours a week, and again, Diana experienced a record-breaking year in billings.

Okay, you're muttering, *isn't that nice. You have babysitters and live-in childcare to watch your kid—I don't.* And therein lies the truth: If you're a parent and have young children, the odds are not in your favor that you'll be able to maintain a full-time freelance career with zero support. You can put your writing career on hold for a couple years. You can decide to work part-time and squeeze assignments in when you can. But if you really want to write full time, you're probably going to have to make some serious accommodations. No one said it's easy, but you *can* work full time and raise children even if you're a freelancer.

If you want to continue building your career and you have no idea how to work around your children, here are some options to consider:

Ask a family member or trusted neighbor to watch your child.

Some lucky freelancers have a parent or in-law nearby who can watch their children for free or cheap; Linda and her family moved to North Carolina in part to be near her parents, who watched her preschooler son a couple days per week so Linda could work. You could also try working out an arrangement with a neighbor or another local writer; for example, she watches your child for three hours on Monday morning and you watch her child for three hours Friday afternoon.

Put your child in daycare.

Millions of working parents do it. There are some excellent daycares and early childhood education programs; research shows young children reap benefits in a dynamic environment. The bad news: Good day care is pricy. Linda used to pay $600 per month to have her son, who was a toddler at the time, in daycare two days per week.

Hire babysitters or a nanny.

If you're nervous about leaving your child with a sitter, take solace in the fact that you'll probably be working in another room rather than in a cubicle twenty miles away.

Mine downtime ruthlessly.

Kids take naps. They zone out in front of the TV. They play with other children on the playground. This is all time you can use to work on your career. One education writer Diana knows gets up at 5:00 a.m. and works three hours until her two sons awaken. Her husband takes over in the evening, and she squeezes in another few hours of work. She schedules interviews during naptimes or when she has a babysitter over. That's roughly 30 hours a week, and she's supporting her family on her income while her husband builds a new business. Pretty impressive!

You can absolutely build a freelance career with limited childcare. Lynne Ticknor, a Maryland-based freelancer and mother of four, specializes in articles on parenting and family life. In the beginning, she had no childcare. "For the first year or more," she says, "my work hours were 5:30 am to 7:30 am before the kids woke up and 1:30 pm to 3:30 pm while the baby, whose sleep habits were extremely predictable, napped and the older kids were in school. That gave me 20 hours a week to work, excluding weekends and evenings. I was able to break into national consumer magazines working those hours."

Sometimes she was able to hire a sitter while she conducted phone interviews or had meetings with editors, but she tried to schedule those appointments during evening hours. In fact, she found many sources who preferred to be interviewed during the evening when her husband could watch the kids. Says Ticknor, "It sure wasn't easy getting up at the crack of dawn every day, but it allowed me to build my writing career part time without putting my children in daycare." Building her freelancing business has taken a lot of sacrifice: She doesn't get to spend as much time as she would like with her husband, and cleaning, cooking, and doing laundry get short shrift. As she says, "In order to find the time to work, something has to give!" So out with scrubbing tubs and in with polishing prose.

Look: Whether it's kids, a sick spouse, or an aging parent, everyone has personal obstacles that make building and maintaining a writing career seem impossible. If you're committed to building a career and you have these kinds of responsibilities on your shoulders, you simply have to be more ruthless and creative about your time than other writers. In fact, by developing your hidden resources, you'll probably become a better, more successful writer than those people whose biggest life problem is deciding between a Netflix show or an Amazon movie on a Thursday night.

Write for content mills to gain clips and experience.

Content sites, a.k.a. content mills, are popular among new writers as a way to rack up clips and earn some quick cash. These sites accept all sorts of articles and pay low—like $10 per article low—but fast. Many beginning writers accept the crappy pay in the name of "paying their dues," but there's a difference between paying your dues and playing the sucker.

First of all, the assertion that you can use articles published on these content sites as clips is absurd. Many of the articles are exercises in jamming keywords into copy, and even the ones that aren't tend to be low quality. (What do you expect when writers are trying to churn out multiple articles per day to keep the lights on?) The difference between a content site and a legit publication is like the difference between wearing a T-shirt with the Harvard logo on it and graduating with a degree from Harvard. Anyone with $15 can buy and wear the T-shirt, but getting the genuine sheepskin for your wall will take more effort.

Second, writers often defend their content mill habit by claiming they can whip out an article for a content site in an hour, which means they're probably not doing research, interviewing sources, fact checking their work, or writing to the best of their abilities. However, editors at high-paying pubs require those exact skills, so sending them clips that lack these elements isn't the smartest move.

If you feel the need to work your way up the publishing ladder, why not start out with small, regional publications, your local newspaper, or trade publications? (More about these later in the book.) These publications pay anywhere from five cents to a dollar or more per word, which is more than you'll get from many content sites. More importantly, these publications require better research and writing of their writers and boast more rigorous editing, giving you better-looking clips in addition to a decent amount of dough.

Check the newsstands for magazines to pitch.

This "rule" can be depressing for new writers who notice how many of their favorite print magazines have been going under in recent years. How can you make a living as a magazine writer when there are hardly any magazines left?

The good news is, the magazines on your local newsstand are a minuscule percentage of the markets that exist and that hire freelance writers. Here are some other options you can try:

Trade Magazines

Trade magazines are business-to-business publications for readers in particular industries. You can find trades for every (and we mean every) industry, from window washing to large-scale printing. Case in point: Linda recently read an announcement for a new trade magazine dealing in dung management. Her husband Eric has written for *International Fiber Journal, Indian Gaming Business*, and *Sheep!* magazines. And when Diana wrote advertising copy for a bandage manufacturer, she subscribed to *Journal of Burn Care and Rehabilitation.*

Trades can be also a good place to break into magazine writing if you don't have any publishing credits yet. You can pitch trade magazines that relate to your job, education, or hobby, which will give you an automatic "in."

Custom Publications

Custom publications are magazines created by content companies for corporate clients and organizations. (Content companies also create and run blogs, newsletters, and more for their clients.) For example, the magazine you receive if you're a Wells Fargo business customer is a custom publication. The magazine the cashier sticks in your grocery bag if you spend $50 at Hannaford supermarkets is a custom publication. The magazine you'll find at your American Taekwondo Association-affiliated martial arts studio? You got it—custom published.

Many customer publishers exist, and some companies that produce consumer magazines, like Meredith (which publishes *Fitness* and *Family Circle*), also have a custom publishing division. Custom publishers often pay on par with newsstand magazines; for example, the custom pubs we've written for often pay $1.00 per word and up.

Writing for a custom publication is very similar to writing for a newsstand magazine; for example, you need to interview sources and write in a style that fits the magazine. However, you may be expected to mention the client's products in your articles, interview the client's customers as sources, or even let the client sources approve their quotes.

You can often break into a custom publication by sending a letter of introduction to the editor. Even better, if that editor likes you, he's likely to recommend you to editors of other pubs the company produces. Making our writerly lives easier is the fact that The Content Council website has a directory of custom publishers with links to their sites.

Online Publications

While many print publications have online counterparts, you'll also find many online-only magazines that hire freelance writers. For example, Bankrate.com uses freelancers to write finance articles, and Everyday Health pays for health-related pieces. You can pitch them using many of the same methods you'd use for print publications. (More on marketing of all types, from query letters to social media, in Chapter 3, "No-Fear Marketing.")

In-House Publications

Some businesses and organizations put out their own magazines without the help of a custom publisher; many alumni magazines are examples of this.

Blogs

Some blogs do pay! And Linda has found her magazine writing background helpful for snagging paying blog assignments, because blog owners are deluged with so many off-topic, shoddily written guest post pitches that they gratefully welcome Linda's well-written, well-researched pitch letters.

In short, look beyond the newsstand and you'll find a plethora of paying markets for freelance writers.

You need "connections" to land assignments.

We think you're confusing breaking into writing with breaking into Hollywood, or maybe with making it big in multi-level marketing.

When Linda started freelancing in 1997, she didn't even know the janitors at any of the publications she was pitching, much less the editors. All the wonderful "connections" she has today came from good, hard work. Diana happened to know the editor who assigned her first article with *Connecticut Magazine*, but after that, she targeted and broke into magazines where she knew no one on staff.

We're not going to lie and tell you connections won't help you; they will. If you have an "in" with an editor, your proposal may get priority, or you may even have an assignment thrown your way. But what's more valuable to you, and to any editor—whether she's someone you played bridge with in college or a complete stranger—are your timely ideas and professional attitude. These two attributes will take you further than the connections lesser writers gnash their teeth over.

If you're still not convinced, don't worry: The connections you desire are simple to make. So simple, in fact, that we scratch our heads whenever we hear some poor new writer railing about another writer's success due to his friends in high places.

Here's the deal. Say you email several pitches over a period of several months to a publication. One day, instead of sending you yet another form rejection, the editor finally writes back and says, "Sorry, we already have that article in progress with another writer, but feel free to send me more ideas." Bingo—you've got yourself a connection. The next time you pitch her, you can write, "Thanks for inviting me to send you more ideas...."

But many writers don't consider that sort of interaction a *connection*, and they completely blow it off. They feel a connection is someone who calls them and says something like, "Hey, remember me from that bar crawl in '10? I'm a magazine editor now and I hear you're a writer. Feel like covering the cocktail scene in Paris for us?" (That's a total fantasy, by the way.) If you're a good writer with lots of salable ideas, we assure you—you will soon have more editorial connections than you'll know how to handle.

Here are other ways smart writers develop connections:

They keep in contact with editors who change jobs.

Diana, for example, worked with a terrific editor at *Psychology Today*. When the editor changed jobs and went to *Parenting*, Diana suddenly had an "in" at a magazine she'd been trying to crack for a long time. She became a frequent contributor to the magazine for many years and followed the editor to *Kiwi* when she became editor-in-chief.

They send introductory emails.

Editors are conditioned to ignore the pile of submissions on their desks, but they will often respond to a friendly email. This won't always work, but why not give it a try? Linda once sent an intro letter to fifteen editors at top magazines asking for details on what they were looking for—*not* selling herself or pitching an idea—and received personal, encouraging replies from *Shape*, *Health*, and *Better Homes & Gardens*.

They meet with editors.

If you really want to make a personal connection, next time you're in New York (or near a publication's office elsewhere), ask an editor out for coffee. Even if they know you only from rejecting your pitches, many editors will respond favorably to such a request. Often, once they see you're a witty, charming, intelligent coffee companion, they'll be even more receptive to your proposals.

When Linda lived in New England, she'd make an annual trek to New York City to meet with editors at *Family Circle*, *Redbook*, *Fitness*, and other publications. And whenever she had a road trip planned she'd research what publishers were located along the way, which led her to meet editors at Rodale in Pennsylvania and Imagination Publishing in Chicago.

They ask editors for introductions.

There's nothing wrong with approaching an editor at Magazine A with whom you have good rapport and asking if she knows an editor at Magazine B who would be receptive to a proposal. If she does give you a name, consider this an awesome connection—you can start your pitch with, "My editor at Magazine A gave me your name...."

In addition, if the magazine you're writing for has sister publications, ask your editor to introduce you to the editors at these other titles. When Linda mentioned to her editor at *Men's Fitness* that she had an idea for the magazine's sister publication, *Muscle & Fitness Hers*, her editor actually walked over to this magazine's editorial offices and passed her name on to the editors there. Soon, Linda had an assignment to write about alternative therapies for *Muscle & Fitness Hers*.

They socialize with other writers.

It's classic "you scratch my back and I'll scratch yours." Linda and Diana, along with several other writers in their circle, regularly trade leads, contact names, and other valuable information. After Linda shared the name of one of her editors with another writer, for example, the writer responded with the contact info of an editor for a new teen magazine.

BREAK THIS RULE

You have to live in New York City to succeed.

Of all the successful freelance writers we know, only a handful live close to the editor nexus known as Manhattan. Diana lives in Boston, Linda lived in New England and then North Carolina, and we know writers who live in Kentucky, Kansas, California, and even Greece, Australia, India, and England. We've even met a few writers who live year-round in RVs! In fact, the farther away you live from your editors, the more valuable you can be to them, because you can deliver stories and a perspective they won't find on Madison Avenue.

What's more, not every publication has a New York-based editorial staff. *Shape*, for example, is based in Los Angeles, *Southern Living* and *Coastal Living* are in Alabama, and *The Atlantic*'s editorial offices were in Boston for years, but are now located in DC. Location may be all-important in real estate, but you're selling ideas, not land—and ideas can be written about from anywhere.

Stop worrying that you can't make it big as a writer if you're not in New York. You can succeed in writing from anywhere, except if you're totally off the grid.

BREAK THIS RULE

You need to spend a lot of money
to get your freelance career off the ground.

Let's see, you'll need a home office, a laptop, a printer/scanner/copier combo, a high-speed internet connection, accounting software, full-color business cards, a professionally designed website...

Stop! Really, if you needed all this stuff, you'd have to slave at your day job nigh unto Doomsday to pay for it. Sure, having a fully equipped office would be nice, but when you're starting out, you need only the basics, especially if you're making a leap of faith into freelancing without a load of assignments in the pipeline already. If you are one of these brave souls, any extra money jingling in your pockets should be going toward life's little essentials like food, clothing, and shelter.

Even if you're lucky enough to have a partner or spouse footing your freelance apprenticeship, there's no need to go wild at the office supply store. Editors want nothing more than good ideas presented professionally, so ditch the four-color business cards and fancy website. At first, all you really need is access to a computer with an internet connection. If you're strapped for cash, reserve computer time at the local library and invest in this equipment as soon as your cash flow improves. You don't even need the most recent edition of that freelancing bible, *Writer's Market*, because most every public library has a copy.

Diana used the proceeds from her first-ever magazine sale to purchase a 486 desktop PC (the best at the time), a Hewlett-Packard inkjet printer, and Microsoft Word. In case you're wondering, no, the amount she was paid didn't cover the cost of all these goodies, but she was still working at her marketing job at the time. She upgraded her PC several times since then and now works on a Mac laptop. (For the record, it is now 2017 and she's still working on her 2008 MacBook because she's too cheap to buy a new computer.) For letterhead (since in those days you usually snail mailed your pitches), she set up a template in Word with her contact information above a solid line break. As for business cards, she had 500 black and white ones professionally printed ($30) once she began meeting with editors. Her first office? A Queen Anne-style desk set up in the corner of her bedroom.

Honestly, the start-up costs for a writing career can be quite modest. What *can* be expensive, however, is a wage-slave lifestyle footed by a freelance income.

Say you've started getting assignments from editors while working a full-time job, and you decide to quit to write full time. Paychecks from a company come regularly, once a week or twice a month. But magazines don't work this way, unless you're on staff. Diana's first article for *Connecticut Magazine*, for example, was assigned in the spring, but the deadline for copy wasn't until September. The editors then took another month to edit and approve her article, and then Diana had to wait an additional 30 days for payment, as specified in the contract. Her check finally arrived in time for the first snows of December. A lot of rent payments and utility bills came due between the assignment and its check.

Linda has actually waited more than a year for one of her articles to be "accepted" by the publication that assigned it! Unfair, yes; uncommon, no.

The bottom line: Save the money you think you need to spend on apps, business cards, and pro website design, and learn how to live on less. Experts generally advise entrepreneurs to stockpile enough cash to finance three to six months of living expenses, and we recommend leaning towards the half-year figure—despite Linda's speedy success—because nothing brings on a case of writer's block faster than the sound of your last dollars being sucked out of your checking account. Desperation rarely begets inspiration.

Follow publications' writers' guidelines.

A few years after Linda started writing for magazines, she realized she had amassed an entire box full of guidelines she had never looked at. Reading the magazine, looking up the publication online or in *Writer's Market*, and calling to verify the editor's name gave her all the information she needed—and that situation hasn't changed. In fact, an editor at a major women's magazine once told Linda that the editors rarely even know what's in their guidelines; they're there to scare off the less-than-serious, and thereby help allay the pressure on the editors' inboxes.

Diana also rarely looks at guidelines anymore. When she started freelancing in 1999, she compiled a stack of them in a three-ring binder that she has since misplaced—and not once has she gone looking for it. The game of musical chairs at most magazines makes guidelines pretty useless in her opinion: New editors like to shake things up and change direction faster than they can update the guidelines.

What she finds more useful is sitting at a bookstore café with the latest issue of a magazine she wants to write for and pretending she's an editor in an assigning mood. What kind of stories does the magazine seem to favor—first-person viewpoint, lots of reporting, or a wealth of expert quotes? She can also tell a lot by looking at the masthead. Are freelancers writing the majority of articles or are staffers?

Often Diana will get a dozen good ideas to pitch from that half-hour of brainstorming. If she's interested in writing for one of the magazine's departments, she simply calls the editorial office when she gets home and asks who assigns for that section.

Don't let this fake rule keep you from pitching the publications you really want to write for. Polish your idea, come up with a compelling pitch, and send it in the way that works best for you. (More on pitching options in Chapter 3.)

BREAK THIS RULE

Never write for free/cheap.

For years we've been preaching to new writers: Know what you're worth! Demand to be paid fairly! Don't write for free!

And now here we are, telling you it's *good* to write for free. Are we crazy?

No. We changed because *the industry* has changed. When we were starting out in the late 1990s, there were no content mills and bidding sites offering writers $15 per 750 words, or blogs paying $20 for an extensive post.

So when we said, "Don't write for free," we meant, "You should be snagging $500 for a feature article." Not, "Don't write for free...at least get a few pennies for your efforts."

Also, in the late 1990s, there was a lot less competition and even a newbie writer had a chance to break into big markets and land impressive clients. Today, thanks to the internet, the competition is stiff and writers with more samples have a better chance of landing gigs. Another reason many aspiring writers flock to the el cheapo clients: "What an easy way to get samples!" they crow.

The bad news is, better-paying writing clients don't take seriously samples from content mills, bidding sites, or amateur-looking blogs. There's no barrier to entry, writers need to crank out words too fast to do their best work, and even a great writer's work is surrounded by mediocre writing from other cheap scribes. (When it comes to clips we always say, "You gotta use what you got," so if clips from content mills are all you have, definitely use them—but certainly *don't* go out of your way to write for these sites for the clips.)

So we're changing our stance on the whole issue:

> *We believe it's better to write for free or cheap temporarily, on your own terms, than to write for pennies for a content mill or bidding site client that doesn't value your skills—and won't make a good sample anyway.*

We've become big fans of writing for nothing, or close to nothing. Here's why.

1. It feels good.

As you'll see below, we recommend writing for free for causes you care about. For example, several years ago Linda was a volunteer writer for the SPCA's newsletter. That's gotta feel way better than writing gratis for some company that hopes to earn lots of profit from your free work.

2. You get to choose your clients.

Landing free gigs is much easier than pitching low-paying clients. After all, the first is, "Hey, I'd love to write a post for you for free to help build my portfolio" (who can say no to that?), and the second is, "You say I'm competing against hundreds of writers for this low-paying assignment? Let me bend over further for you, my liege."

When it comes to getting those first samples or building your reputation in a new field, free is more of a sure thing.

3. You can make demands.

When you're writing for free or offering your writing at a discount, you have more control over what you'll do and what you'll get in return for your efforts. Of course, your client will have standards and specs you'll need to adhere to, but you have more leeway to ask for a byline, negotiate the deadline, or request PDFs of your work.

4. Your writing will kick butt.

When you're writing for a cause or business you love, on a reasonable timeline, you get the chance to show off your creativity, writing skills, and ability to generate ideas. Those are the kinds of samples you want in your portfolio.

5. You only need to do it a few times.

With the content mills, bidding sites, and blogs that pay dismal rates, it's easy to fall into the trap of churning out assignment after assignment, because the only way to make good money is to write in volume.

Soon, you've forgotten that you only started writing for cheap to get a few samples, and are caught in the vicious cycle of mill work. And the longer you do it, the harder it is to climb out.

When you choose to write for free or cheap to get clips, and go into it with your eyes wide open, you're able to set limits on how much you'll do. For example, you may decide you want to become a pet blogger, so you'll write for free for two animal-related nonprofits and your local independent pet supply store, and then use those samples to go after well-paying pet gigs.

When You Should Write for Free

Here are the three situations where you may want to offer your writing services gratis.

1. You have no samples at all.

You're a rank newbie and have zero writing credits to your name. In this case, it makes sense to do a few free gigs to build your portfolio.

2. You're looking to break into a new field.

Say you're a health writer but you'd like to write more about entrepreneurship. You have plenty of samples showing you can write fluently about gluten intolerance and the dangers of Crossfit, but when it comes to business writing—you're starting from scratch. This is a good time to write for free.

3. You want to switch things up.

Maybe you've written dozens of blog posts or brochures or case studies, but you've never written an article—and in your heart you really, really want to become a magazine writer.

Magazine writing is an entirely different skill, and you'll need to prove you've got what it takes. Do a little writing gratis or at a discount and soon you'll have samples to show to paying markets.

4. The article will promote a product or service of yours.

Here's an example: Diana once pitched an idea to a trade magazine. The editor called to assign the piece, and when he offered a ridiculously low rate, she almost laughed in his ear. But before she could seal the fate of the deal with a guffaw, she realized this assignment would generate excellent publicity for the book you're holding in your hands, so she bit back her laughter and took the assignment.

Who to Bestow Your Free/Cheap Writing On

The last thing you want to do is offer the gift of your writing to some greedy conglomerate that's going to turn around and make thousands off it—in other words, a business that can actually afford to pay writers well. That's a sure recipe for resentment. Instead, try approaching:

1. Non-profits.

Chances are, there's a cause you believe in that has a non-profit organization attached to it. Even better, many charities run newsletters or magazines that will let you hone your article writing skills. Check out charities, and their ratings, at Charity Navigator or Charity Watch.

Linda offered her writing services to the Massachusetts Society for the Prevention of Cruelty to Animals and provided articles for their newsletter gratis (until they hired an in-house writer to take over the job). Not only did the experience give Linda pet-related clips—which later turned into assignments from *Cats* magazine and *WebMD*—but she soon noticed that paying work was flowing in faster than ever.

2. Local small businesses you frequent and love.

That little shop downtown that sells handmade soaps, your local co-op grocery store, and the café you visit three days per week that serves farm-to-table cuisine—these can make great prospects for your free writing. Offer to write blog posts or newsletter articles, which are closer to magazine articles than, say, sales letters or press releases.

3. Friends and relatives who are getting their businesses off the ground.

This is a super way to gain writing samples while helping your loved ones. And, they're the most likely of all the types of clients to give you free rein on your work, and to talk you up to potential (paying) writing clients!

4. Hyper-local magazines.

Does your town (or any other small towns near you) have a magazine? Many of these tiny pubs can't pay and will gratefully accept articles from local writers. Check the magazine racks outside of local businesses for these magazines.

5. Yourself.

Got a subject you're passionate about like fruitcake, nail art, or building furniture from junkyard scraps? Start a blog about it and write passionately (and well) on the subject. When you pitch an idea about the subject to magazines, you can ask the editors to check out your blog. If your blog is well-written and interesting, believe us, editors will not only be impressed with your writing, they'll assume you know your stuff more than an unknown freelancer who happened upon this good idea.

What You Get From All This

You're not writing for free for your health...you want something out of the deal. Of course, you'll get samples. But also be sure to request:

1. Credit.

A byline on an article, blog post, or newsletter article will give your sample more credence.

2. Testimonials.

Let your client know that in exchange for your writing, you'd like them to write a testimonial you can run on your website and use in your pitches.

3. Recommendations.

Ask the client if they can recommend you to any of their colleagues—preferably ones who pay writers.

4. Goodies.

Diana once wrote book reviews for a website because she got free mystery and romance novels out of the deal!

Don't Do It Forever

Then—stop! Once you have two or three samples, it's time to stop writing for free and extra-cheap, and use those clips to land high-paying gigs. After all, now you can say, "I've written attention-grabbing articles for X, Y, and Z." That's what you were after, and now you have it.

Offering your writing skills for free or a low price—if you choose the right clients and do a great job—can lead to writing work that pays so well, you're not even tempted to bother with the content mills, bidding sites, and junky blogs. While the "never write for free or cheap" rule worked well in the late 1990s, these days it can pay to bend it.

BREAK THIS RULE

Don't write "shorts" for a magazine if you want to break into the "feature well."

Many writers have very strong opinions about writing "shorts," those 200- to 500-word articles found mostly at the front of a magazine. (These are also known as "FOBs," for "Front of Book.") Some freelancers won't touch them, claiming they're too much work for not enough pay, or that once you're pegged as a "shorts writer" by a magazine, you'll have a hard time convincing that magazine's editors you can handle more complicated stories.

Other freelancers claim that shorts writing is an excellent way to crack a target publication, and that once you've bonded with the assigning editor, she'll be more receptive to pitches for longer stories.

Our take? It depends. We lean toward the pro-shorts side if you're a new freelancer or if you've had no luck interesting an editor in longer story pitches. Some magazines even insist on starting new-to-them writers on shorter pieces before giving them feature work. After all, if a new writer messes up a 200-word short, the resulting hole in the magazine isn't that big. If, on the other hand, that same writer messes up a 2,000-word piece, the editor suddenly has four pages to fill.

Diana went through this process with *Contract Professional*; they gave her a few department pieces at first, but once she proved herself a dependable, straightforward writer, the editor started assigning her 1,500- to 2,500-word features and cover stories.

Also, most magazines have more shorts than features, which means more opportunities for freelancers willing to think small (unless, of course, the shorts are staff-written).

Now, the flip side. Yes, you could be pegged as a shorts writer by your editor—that's the chance you take if you follow this strategy. You can protect yourself with these steps:

1. Don't keep pitching short stuff.

You reap what you sow, so if you continually pitch 200-word news items, you're encouraging the editor to pigeonhole you as an FOB writer.

2. As you write longer stories for other publications (especially competing pubs), send the clips to your editor with a friendly note.

No one likes to be poached from, and we wager your editor will soon call with a bigger assignment.

3. If, despite all this, you sense that you're not making progress with the assigning editor, cut bait and move on.

If she calls with a short, fast assignment, decline it and tell her you've decided to concentrate on longer features. This may be the last time you hear from her, but on the other hand, it could be the kick in the jumpseat that she needs. Kelly James went through this "thanks for thinking of me, but..." process with her editors, and a few of them did stop calling to offer shorts. "But not doing them freed me up to pitch, research, and write features which pay much better, so it was worth it in the end," she says. Linda went through the same process with a trade magazine; she told the editor, "It's just not cost-efficient for me to write 250-word pieces." This may sound blunt, but she knew this editor well, and the editor started assigning Linda 1,000-word profiles instead.

If you're a more experienced freelancer, we suggest skipping the "shorts-to-feature" route with new-to-you pubs because there are better ways to get noticed—but don't rule out shorts completely. If you've been pitching features to a target magazine with no luck, and then one day an editor calls with a quick 300-word assignment, it could be time to bite the bullet. For example, Linda's husband Eric submitted a pitch to *Woman's Day* for a feature article on ways to honor your country. The editor liked the idea, but asked Eric to write the idea as a short sidebar that could be appended to an already-scheduled article about volunteering. Eric said yes and later landed longer assignments from this editor.

Also, if you've written longer features for a publication, and then they ask you to do a short, why not take the assignment? If you're a fast writer, the short will take only a couple of hours of work, and if you can get a good per-word rate, the hourly rate can be excellent. For example, 300 words at $1 per word = $300. $300 divided by approximately two hours of research and writing time = $150 per hour. Not too shabby! The point is, instead of automatically saying no to FOBs, decide for yourself whether they're worth your time depending on the situation.

A bad day of freelancing beats a good day at the office.

Many writers harbor this unspoken rule that freelancing is always a better option than a 9-5 job working for an employer. More freedom! Get up when you want! Five-second commute to the office! You control your pay!

However, we need to give you a fair warning that it's not all rainbows, flowers, and unicorns. Despite our advice on how to make the leap from employee to business owner, sometimes freelancing stinks. If you're contemplating the freelance life, remove your rose-tinted glasses and read on for the downsides so you can make an informed decision on whether to quit your day job to write:

No company health insurance plan.

Most working people take health insurance for granted; not freelancers. Obamacare (at the time of this writing!) has made it easier for the self-employed to find a health insurance plan, but it's still going to be a lot more expensive than plans you could get if you were working for a big company that subsidizes health care costs, and that offers perks like contributions to an employee's HFSA (Healthcare Flexible Spending Account), which allows you to pay for certain healthcare costs with pre-tax dollars.

No company-sponsored retirement plan.

401(k) plans, where employers often match your retirement contributions, are for employees; if you want to put aside money for retirement, you'll have to set up an IRA (Individual Retirement Account), Keogh, or SEP (Simplified Employee Pension), and remember to contribute to it regularly. No automatic deductions for you!

Higher taxes.

When you're an employee, your employer pays half of your Social Security tax. As a freelancer, you have to come up with the entire 15 percent on your own.

No paid vacation or sick days.

Can't work because you're laid low with the flu? Too bad, you don't get paid. Want to go on vacation for a week or two? Hope you don't mind taking a pay cut, because you don't get those two weeks per year of paid vacation time like your non-freelance brethren.

No office supplies.

When you work for someone else, all those pens and sticky notes are provided by the Office Supply Fairy. When you're freelance, you have to break out a tutu and wings and become your own Fairy. All those supplies—not to mention the computer, printer, paper clips, business cards, internet access, ink cartridges, paper, and cell phone plan—come from your magic wand. These goodies are tax deductible, but that's small consolation when they used to be free.

No water cooler chitchat.

Unless you've got a setup like Linda has with her work-at-home husband, forget Friday morning gabfests in the company kitchenette about who got kicked off *Project Runway*. Even if you hate working in an office, working at home often gets very lonely—so lonely that you can suddenly find yourself down at the local coffee shop making small talk with any warm body who gets within five feet of your chai.

We're not trying to turn anyone off of freelancing, but we do think you should understand the risks before taking the leap. If we didn't manage to find ways past all these negative issues, we'd never have become freelancers. Once you're making a certain level of income, paying the higher premiums for health insurance, doling out your own cash to stock up the home office, and looking for new ways to stay connected are infinitely preferable to working in someone else's cubicle (at least in our opinions!).

BREAK THIS RULE

Don't quit your day job.

This is a "rule" we hear from all those wannabe freelancers who were afraid to take the leap, well-meaning relatives who worry about us, and writers who weren't able to make it work and ended up back in cubicles. However well-intentioned it may be, it's simply false.

If you really want to freelance full time and you're aware of the pros *and* the cons, you *have* to make the leap. In fact, in a business climate where company job security has largely vanished, you may be better off drumming up your own business than depending on a faceless corporation for your living—a faceless corporation that can turn off 100 percent of your income with little or no warning.

Before making the move to full-time freelancing, make sure you have enough money in the bank to survive for at least six months. When Linda decided to leave her part-time office job to freelance full time, she and her husband salted away enough money to cover only three months worth of expenses, which was plenty since they had no kids, no mortgage, and not even a car payment to worry about. Now that we're ten years older since we last revised this book, we say to aim for nine to 12 months!

Author and writer Brett Forrest says that when he left his fact-checking job, his colleagues at *Men's Journal* asked him, "Are you insane?" By the time he'd given his notice, he had written a few features for the magazine, and he'd made inroads with publications like *Rolling Stone*.

Forrest says the first few months were a challenge. He was living in Manhattan's Lower East Side in a rent-by-month/week/day studio that he shared with a bunch of other writer and editor friends. "The floors slanted and there were cigarette burns all over the carpets from past tenants," he says. "We called it 'the Flophouse.'"

He adds, "It is funny and charming to talk about now, but it was a low point for me. The lowest point came when I walked across the street to this Dominican deli to buy a quarter pound of salami—the cheapest meat they had. I counted out my coins and realized I was a nickel short. I didn't have another nickel on me. The woman who worked there said, 'Oh, I see you here all the time. You can pay me back tomorrow. I know you're good for it.' I hoarded that salami for three days. At that time, I was barely even surviving."

But times got better for Forrest. He started lining up two or three assignments every month, generating enough income to move to a new apartment. In the years since, he's written not only for *Rolling Stone*, but also for *Details*, *Spin*, *Vanity Fair*, *National Geographic*, *The Atlantic*, and *The New York Times Magazine*.

Roxanne Nelson worked as a nurse when she started out freelancing. But then a car accident in 1996 prevented her from working for six months. "I was forced to really forge ahead with my writing career if I wanted to eat and pay rent," she says. "By the time I was well enough to work, I decided that I couldn't bear the thought of it. It was a little bit of a struggle, but I was determined to be a writer and never work as a nurse again. And I've never returned to nursing."

So don't let the naysayers hold you back with this killjoy "rule." If you have a cushion to fall back on—money in the bank and/or a partner who's willing to support you through some lean times—and motivation in spades to make this freelancing life a reality, then go for it! It probably won't be easy, but living off your writing isn't as impossible as others would have you believe.

BREAK THIS RULE

Be a rule-breaker and break all the rules!

This whole book is about when and why you should break rules—and now we're telling you not to break them after all. Are we hypocrites, or merely forgetful?

Neither. We want to make sure you don't get so crazy with the rule breaking that you sabotage your writing career. Plenty of rules, both written and unwritten, will serve you well, so don't go out of your way to break them on principle.

For example, a few of our readers have, without our permission, used our names when pitching to editors at magazines we write for—thereby breaking the rule that you don't drop names without asking first. That's not renegade, that's rude.

Before you can break the rules, you have to understand them. Read up on the freelance writing business in books, in magazines, and online. Follow the rules that make sense to you, and trash those that don't. Every once in a while—maybe every quarter or every six months—sit down and review your writing progress. Have you been following certain rules that are holding you back? What would the consequences be if you ditched them? Are there any rules you've been breaking that you should reinstate? Maybe your attempts to get creative with capitalization à la e.e. cummings have editors less than enthralled? Not every rule is made to be broken.

Melody Warnick

Melody Warnick broke the rules when she sold an article idea to *Next Step* magazine.

How did you come up with your article idea?

I pitched "Stand Out Without Sucking Up," about how and why you should get to know your college professors, to *Next Step* Magazine, which is distributed to more than 18,000 high schools in the U.S., Canada, and Asia. The idea came fairly organically; my husband was applying to grad school and hitting up his old profs for recommendations, and I complained that I had never gotten to know my profs well enough to feel comfortable asking for that kind of thing. Writing the article was simply my way of passing along some handy, wish-I-had-done-that advice to high school juniors and seniors.

Your query was longer than usual. What info did you include?

To be honest, it was one of the first queries I had ever sent. But I had suffered from the typical freelance delusion that people were going to steal my work if I offered too much info, so I had sent another query to a different magazine where I barely hinted at what the content would be. In this pitch, I just laid it all out, including 3 of the 5 bullet points that I planned to cover in the article, along with two paragraphs of introductory anecdotes. Not counting my bio, the query was 435 words, about half of what the final article was. (It was also the first time I attempted to get some quotes before I had an assignment, though I ended up sending the query without them anyway.)

Did you do any negotiating with the editor?

The contract they sent me was work-for-hire; all rights remained with the publication. Though I was a newbie freelancer, I had done enough reading to know that I wanted to keep the copyright if possible.

Because it was the first time working with this publication, I wasn't sure if it would be overstepping bounds to try and renegotiate the contract, but I figured they couldn't tell that I wasn't a seasoned pro, and I simply emailed the editor saying that I preferred to sell first North American serial rights, and would that be possible? She quickly agreed, with the clause that I couldn't resell the article to any of the magazine's direct competitors (she named a few). Who knows if I'll ever use the material again anyway—it's fairly specialized—but it was incredibly empowering to succeed with that and realize that editors often are open to negotiation, they'll just automatically offer their worst contract first.

How did you get started as a writer?

You probably don't want to hear about my short story experiments as a second grader, but I've written for myself for a long time. Placing in a very competitive personal essay contest at my university, though, helped me realize that I actually had the goods to write for others. Over the years I had published a few personal essays here and there, but it wasn't until this fall that I did some research about queries and pitched an article to a regional magazine. Getting a positive response was about the coolest thing that ever happened to me. Ironically, the magazine eventually rejected the finished article, but by then I'd already had successes with other pubs.

Do you have any advice for aspiring magazine writers?

The biggest question that kept me (and, I think, most aspiring writers) from starting a freelance career sooner was that age-old question, "How do I get clips if I don't have any?" I wrote a few personal essays and articles for tiny publications that wanted to see the finished product instead of a query with clips. Also, I haven't waited the year or so that it sometimes takes to get an article published before using it as a clip; if a piece has been accepted, I simply send the Word file and describe it as "forthcoming." Although *The Renegade Writer* tells you to shoot for the top, I personally have had better luck with the little guys; once I have a handful of clips that I'm proud of, then I'll start working on the national consumer mags.

One final bit of advice: do your research. I've read lots of books on freelancing (*The Renegade Writer* being the best, of course), and I hang out at sites like mediabistro.com and writersweekly.com, if only to get a feel for the lingo of the publishing world.

It's been ten years since you spoke to us. How has your career changed?

I've spent the last 10 years trying to baby-step my way through a freelance writing career, and this *Next Step* success was the barest of beginnings. After that, I tried parlaying every publication into another assignment. I was like, "I have a better clip, now I'm going to pitch a higher-paying publication." My pipe dream was to break into a magazine that my mom could buy on a grocery store newsstand in Spokane, and eventually I did, with *Parenting*. Then the *Parenting* clip opened doors at other national magazines.

Honestly, it wasn't just the clips. I became more skilled at pitching and writing, and I had editors take me with them when they moved magazines. I also slowly moved niches, from parenting to personal finance to human interest. In the past ten years I've written for *Reader's Digest*, *O: The Oprah Magazine*, *Redbook*, *Better Homes and Gardens*, *Ladies' Home Journal*, *Woman's Day*, *Parents*, *American Baby*, and a slew of other magazines and websites. And in 2016, I published my first book, *This Is Where You Belong: The Art and Science of Loving the Place You Live*, which came out from Viking. That was its own amazing, educational experience, so right now I'm teetering between writing more books and going back to magazines, trying to decide where to put my focus over the next few years.

In a nutshell, I'm a little in shock and incredibly grateful at how far I've come in ten years. All of it has been rewarding as heck.

CHAPTER 2

Cranking Up the Idea Factory: Bold Thinking Leads To Countless Ideas

Coming up with salable ideas is all about lying, cheating, and stealing: Lying by writing about topics you know nothing about, cheating by playing games instead of working, and stealing by nabbing topics from government reports, books, and even other articles. Wondering how breaking the rules can turn you into an idea-generating writing machine? Keep reading and we'll tell you.

BREAK THIS RULE

Don't steal ideas.

News flash: Ideas can't be copyrighted, so ideas can't be stolen. Feel free to take ideas that you find and sell them to magazines yourself. Here's a list of buried treasure waiting to be pilfered:

Newsletters.

Linda gets a monthly newsletter from a food safety organization, and one article that caught her eye defined common food additives, such as guar gum, lactic acid, and Yellow #5. Linda pitched that same idea to *Oxygen* magazine—and sold it.

Government reports.

If the U.S. government is good at one thing, it's churning out information, all of which can be mined for article ideas. The website of the U.S. Department of Agriculture, for example, has discussed the national standards for organic foods. What great start for an article idea!

Press releases.

That's why organizations develop press releases: to get press. Say you like to write about science—you can get scientific press releases from Eurekalert.org. You can also ask to be put on the press lists of such organizations as NASA and NOAA (the National Oceanic & Atmospheric Administration).

Trade magazines.

Articles in trade magazines can often be turned into features for a much broader audience. For example, a writer for *Funworld*, which is read by amusement industry professionals, used his bank of industry expertise to sell an article about roller coasters to a large national magazine.

Even if you're not an expert in the fields of microbiology, raising sheep, or call centers, you can often glean ideas from mags devoted to such fields.

Regional magazines and newspapers.

A regional idea may have more far-reaching appeal as well. Many national magazines want stories about exceptional people, successful businesses, and so on, and regional pubs are where these subjects will first appear. Susan Orlean's *New Yorker* essay "Orchid Fever" germinated from a tiny news item in a Florida newspaper. (She later expanded the article into a book, *The Orchid Thief.*)

Consumer magazines.

Okay, you wouldn't want to take an article about forgotten bands of the 1960s from *Rolling Stone* and pitch the idea to its competitor, *SPIN*. But why not pitch a similar idea to *AARP*, a magazine for people over age 50? Or how about an article on 1960s chick-flicks for *Glamour*?

Books.

Magazine editors like topics that are made timely by the publication of a new book, so when Linda spotted the book *Positive Energy* by Judith Orloff, M.D., she pitched one of the ideas Orloff wrote about—intuitive energy—and sold it to *Body + Soul*; a new book on resilience spawned an article for *Oxygen*. These book-to-mag transformations gave her ready-made sources on tap: the books' authors.

Also, take creative riffs on books; for example, when Diana caught sight of a bird identification guide during one of her son's tantrums, she put birds and babies together and came up with "a field guide to temper tantrums," which *Parenting* quickly commissioned. She also regularly flips through the psychology and self-help books at bookstores to come up with ideas for relationship articles.

Your own articles.

Once you've done the work of coming up with, selling, researching, and writing an idea, you should get as much mileage out of it as possible. For example, Linda once wrote an article for *Redbook* called "The Better

Orgasm Diet," about foods that boost the libido. She then reslanted the idea for men, queried it, and landed an assignment from *Men's Fitness* called "Vanity Fare," about foods that improve men's hair, breath, and physique to make them more desirable to women. Linda also wrote about ways to trick yourself into eating less for *Oxygen*, then reslanted the idea for *Muscle Media*.

But how can you steal ideas from others without feeling a twinge of guilt—or at least fearing that an editor will realize you pilfered the topic? Here are questions to ask to help you make any idea your own:

How could this writer have done better?

Say you see an article of tips on selling your house that you think is a little weak, because the writer didn't use experts and instead relied on anecdotes from people who successfully sold their homes. Maybe you can pitch a story on "10 Surprising Secrets From the Experts for Selling Your House Fast."

What is the opposite of this topic?

You read an article in a business magazine about unique advertising techniques that work. Why not pitch a story about advertising methods that don't work, or famous ad flops? As another example, Linda once wrote an article about selling to women's magazines for *Writer's Digest* magazine. A few months later, she pitched a story about writing for men's magazines to *The Writer*. Within a week, she had an assignment.

Who else would be interested in this idea?

Eric saw a small piece in *Reader's Digest* about the National Wife-Carrying Championships taking place the following month in Bethel, Maine. Who else would be interested in this news? Game magazines, of course! Eric sold a short piece about the competition to *GAMES*, and snagged a fun, tax-deductible trip to Maine to boot.

How can I make this idea regional?

An article in a cooking magazine about Ethiopian cuisine could be translated into an article about Rhode Island's Ethiopian restaurants for a local magazine.

How can I make this regional idea national?

When Diana picked up her college's alumnae magazine a couple of years ago and read about an etiquette seminar the college sponsored during winter break, she thought the etiquette consultant who ran the seminar would be perfect for a career profile for an online magazine for freelancers—and the magazine thought so, too.

How can I narrow this idea?

If you run across an article in a health magazine about the popularity of martial arts, trim the idea down by pitching an article about how to get started in tae kwan do or krav maga. Linda's own articles about martial arts led her to write a piece for *Fitness* about how karate helped her overcome panic disorder.

How can I broaden this idea?

Linda once wrote an article about how to peel a banana—a very narrow topic. A smart writer could have stolen that idea and turned it into an article on the easiest ways to peel and prepare difficult fruits like pomegranates, pineapple, and mangoes.

Your goal is for editors to send you ideas.

Many writers dream of the day they have such impressive clips and such a giant roster of clients, they can sit back and let editors call them with assignments. No pitching required!

While some editors, such as those at trade magazines, will gladly assign you ideas that were generated in-house, you will be much more valuable to your editors if you take the burden of generating ideas off their shoulders. "While I regularly send out assignments to freelancers, I prefer to get story pitches. There's no mystery why," says a former editor at Bankrate.com. "We have a fairly narrow area in which we work. After you've assigned out 100 or 200 credit card stories, it's a little tough to come up with fresh ideas sometimes. So a bright, clever, useable idea from a freelancer is always appreciated, and generally results in an assignment."

Another thing to consider is that while you *can* find editors who will hand you assignments *sans* pitch (see below), those are usually articles that won't have you singing with excitement, because you didn't come up with the ideas yourself. You'll do them for the money, and that's it. If you want to occasionally write a piece (for pay) on a topic you're passionate about, you'll probably need to pitch.

For example, even though Linda has a roster of clients she works with regularly, she still writes queries when an idea pops into her head she absolutely *has* to write. Most recently, she and her family were appalled at how servers in restaurants would comment on how much they had eaten: "Wow, you cleaned your plates!" or "You didn't like that at all, huh? [wink]" She quickly pitched and sold an idea to *Pizza Today* magazine called "The Final Word," about how servers can graciously end a meal so guests will want to come back.

Pitching may be a pain, but it's a part of the writing profession. Keep on brainstorming ideas for your editors, and you're sure to land more assignments than the writer who waits for a handout—and you'll also get the chance to write about topics that excite you.

BREAK THIS RULE

You need to pitch your butt off forever.

We said above that pitching is part of the freelance writing game, and it is. But if you're one of the many writers who hates marketing, take heart: You won't have to crank out the ideas like a pitching machine forever. When you're first starting out, you'll need to market pretty much every minute you're not working on a paying assignment to gain momentum. However, eventually you'll have at least some clients who come to you with work regularly, so you can relax a bit between assignments.

Always keep a pen and paper on your nightstand to capture great ideas you have at night.

This "rule" presupposes that all writers come up with article ideas in their sleep—and if you don't, there's something wrong with you.

Not everyone comes up with brilliant ideas in bed, although the way the writing books and magazines have it, if you don't have a pen and paper on your nightstand you're throwing away money in your sleep. We've spoken to many writers who say their best ideas come to them while they're driving, shopping, talking to a neighbor, or taking a shower. So don't panic if your nocturnal brain isn't all that brilliant; you can find ideas in other places as well.

Whenever Linda has an idea she doesn't want to get away, she dictates it into an email on her phone, which she always has with her. She's come up with some of her best ideas while grocery shopping, eating at restaurants, and going on long road trips. Diana also uses the recording feature on her smartphone to capture ideas on the fly. (Safety alert: Do not use your smartphone while driving.) She's done everything from dictating ideas into an email that she sends to herself, to opening up an idea file she keeps in her Evernote app; she either voice records the idea or keys it in.

Like many other writers, Diana gets her best ideas in the shower, so she keeps a tube of cheap lipstick handy. Whenever a great idea lathers up, she jots it down on the shower stall wall. When she's all dressed and ready to head downstairs, she transfers her shower jottings into a notebook and scrubs off the lipstick with a shower brush. (If you try this, test the lipstick-and-wall combo first to make sure it doesn't stain.)

Predict what the editor will assign by reading past issues of the publication.

It helps to look to the past for inspiration, but even better is to look to the future via the magazine's editorial calendar. The editorial calendar is a list of the features and themes a magazine plans to publish in the upcoming year. (The editorial calendar is the work of both the editorial and the advertising departments. Editorial will have guidelines for accepting articles, and ad reps will be able to show potential advertisers why they should buy ad space: "June is our annual theme issue on farming llamas and other camelids, and your llama de-fleaing spray will go over great with readers!")

Getting the editorial calendar may be tricky, but it's worth the effort. Since the calendar lists the themes for each issue, you can come up with ideas that fit into the themes and pitch them to the editor. When Eric accessed the editorial calendar for *Playthings* magazine, for example, he saw that one issue would be devoted to board games and puzzles. Bingo! He queried the editor on an article about merchandising board games—something he happened to have a lot of experience in.

To get your hands on an editorial calendar, your first stop is the magazine's website, which may have the calendar posted in the advertisers' section and sometimes with the writers' guidelines.

If that doesn't work, try calling the magazine's advertising department—the number is usually listed in the magazine's masthead. Sometimes the person who answers the phone will send you a calendar no questions asked. But other times, they screen requests to make sure that the editorial calendar goes out only to potential advertisers and not to, say, competitors. In fact, you might want to email the advertising department instead of calling, since they'll be less likely to ask questions.

BREAK THIS RULE

Write what you know.

If Linda could write only about topics that she's had personal experience in, the possibilities would be limited to writing, linguistics, yoga, and parenting. But instead she's taken the idea "Write what you don't know" to heart and has published articles about artificial intelligence, game theory, what astronauts eat on the space shuttle, migrant health care, trolley parks, customer relationship management, natural health care for pets, large-format printing, and much more. She's also co-authored books on becoming a personal trainer, the history of timekeeping, and starting and running a coffee bar.

Linda became a jack-of-all trades early on. In 1997 and 1998, she wrote articles for trade magazines like *QSR* (Quick Service Restaurant) *Success*, *Mini Storage Messenger*, *Pastry Art & Design*, and *Party & Paper Retailer*. She would contact trade magazines with an introduction letter, and they would call her with assignments on a variety of topics. They didn't care that Linda had no experience in these industries because with a pay rate of 30 cents per word or less, these magazines couldn't afford to be picky—they only needed a good writer.

Knowing that she could write about, say, how to create a jicama display or how mini-storage facility owners can hire the best employees gave Linda the confidence to pitch magazines on other subjects she didn't know much about. She soon sold an article about careers in game theory to *American Careers* and a piece about extended-wear contact lenses to *Edge*.

Eventually, Linda built up multiple niches that she could write about with ease: business, science, health, nutrition, careers, pets, women's interest, parenting, and kids' interest.

When it comes to selling articles that are out of your range of experience, success builds on itself. If you start out with the attitude that you can research and write about anything, you will keep landing assignments on topics that are out of your ken. The wider the variety of assignments you complete, the more confident editors will be in assigning you stories on topics in which you have no previous experience. (This is how Eric ended up writing about proper nutrition during pregnancy for *Oxygen*. No uterus required!)

So don't feel you can write only about your own hobbies and personal experiences. Take a chance and branch out by researching ideas that are a stretch for you.

You need to generate lots of new ideas.

New ideas are good, but old ideas can be better. Instead of racking your brain to come up with the Next Big Idea, why not recycle the ones you've already written about? The smart writer tries to get as much as they can out of every idea.

Linda once wrote an article for *Walking* called "The Bitter Truth," about people who are genetically predisposed to hate vegetables. Because she sold only First North American Serial Rights to the magazine, Linda was free to sell the article elsewhere. So she sent it to *Vibrant Life*, which paid her about $150 for the article—not too bad for two minutes' work. She then took the information from the article, condensed it into a much shorter piece, and sold it to *FitnessLink*. A couple of years later, Linda rewrote the idea for *Men's Fitness*.

Linda also sold an article about how to maintain a positive online image to *Business Start-Ups*, and then resold the idea to *Minority Engineer*, CareerMag.com, and *Succeed*. She earned several hundred dollars by rewriting the article for each market. And through a reprint service called Featurewell, which still exists now in 2017, Linda resold a *Family Circle* article on home care at least five times.

Kelly James is the guru of reprints; in fact, she wrote a chapter about reprints for *Trade Secrets: A Professional Guide to the Business of Non-fiction Freelance Writing*, published by the American Society of Journalists and Authors (ASJA). In 2000 she was writing for national magazines but realized there were other markets—primarily smaller mags or regional pubs—that might be interested in her articles, especially the evergreen topics (those topics magazines turn to again and again). "These markets don't pay as much as national mags, but it's essentially 'free' money," she says.

James had a slew of evergreen bridal stories on subjects like getting along with your in-laws, talking about money, and dealing with wedding planning stress, so she searched for regional bridal markets that might want those same pieces. She called the mags, asked if they'd be interested in reprints, and sent packages with sample articles and a list of available story ideas. Then she followed up on them. Using this method, James sold to about a half-dozen bridal markets throughout the country. Some buy only one or two articles, but others have bought many pieces from her over several years.

James then started looking for possible health and fitness reprint markets. This was tougher, but she's found a couple of markets that buy her articles. She contacts them every three to four months to let them know which new stories she has available for reprint.

"I don't know how many articles I've reprinted—I'd guess about 25, but several of those have sold more than once," James says. "My biggest hits have been the bridal ones—a couple of those have sold three or four times, and I continue sending them out when I find new regional markets. I'll also occasionally offer what I call 'tweaks' where I revise the original story for the new market, for example editing a diet story that originally ran in a women's magazine so it's appropriate for a bridal mag. I still consider it a reprint, though, and market it accordingly." In two years James made about $5,000 from reprinted work.

Here's how you can duplicate James's success: When you're assigned an article that you think has the potential to sell to other magazines, do everything you can to get a contract that claims only First North American Serial Rights to the article. This means the magazine has the right to be the first magazine to run your article; after that, the rights to the article revert back to you.

Once your article has been published in the first magazine, use Google, *Writer's Market*, and other directories to find markets that accept reprints. Linda likes to use the online version, WritersMarket.com, because you can search for magazines based on whether they accept reprints. If you use the print version, you'll have to read every magazine entry to find out which ones might buy your previously published work.

Then, create a letter that will make editors drool with anticipation over the idea of reading your article. Here's the letter Linda used to sell reprints of "The Bitter Truth":

> *Dear Ms. Publishme:*
>
> *Look through just about any health magazine and you'll see an article advising its readers to turn to vegetables for their anticancer compounds and disease-fighting fiber. These health benefits are great news for vegetable lovers. But where does that leave those of us who think veggies are vile?*
>
> *There are more of us than you think. In fact, new studies show there is an entire group of people—"supertasters," people who are very sensitive to bitterness—who are likely to scorn veggies.*
>
> *In "The Bitter Truth," I talked with taste researchers and nutritionists to tell veggie-hating readers how to satisfy their nutritional requirements through means other than vegetables and how to really disguise the vegetables in their meals so they can get the nutrients they need and worry less about their health.*
>
> *The first North American rights for "The Bitter Truth" were purchased by Walking magazine and the story appeared in the October issue. I'm offering reprint rights to the piece. Will you share this article with your readers?*

There's no need to mention or include clips, since you're sending the entire article.

BREAK THIS RULE

It's easy to find ideas!
They're everywhere in your life.

We firmly believe that you can pull ideas out of every aspect of your life. So why are we refuting that belief here?

It's true that ideas are everywhere, but sometimes it's tough to catch them as they whiz through your frontal lobes. If you're feeling like you couldn't grab a good idea if it walked up and kicked you in the shins, try these tactics:

Play a game.

Diana, Linda, and Eric came up with a game to rev up the idea-generating process. One of them would throw out a word, and then they'd all try to think up article ideas related to that word. "Green," Diana challenged at their last session. "An inside look at how money is made," Eric offered. "Tips from golf course owners on how to care for your lawn," Linda suggested. "How to deal with friends who are green with envy over your successes," said Diana. Diana ended up selling an article on this last topic to *The Writer*.

Read outside the box.

Another way to overcome writer's block is to check out magazines you wouldn't normally read. Browsing through *Aeronautics Monthly* or *Modern Ferret* not only helps you find fresh ideas you can reslant for other markets, it also introduces you to a whole new world of writers and writing styles. And you can do this anytime you want, gratis, by going to your local bookstore café, gathering up armloads of magazines from sections you rarely peruse, and reading them over a cup of java.

Get a kick in the pants.

Try something you've never tried before. Once when Linda was feeling burned out she signed up for karate classes, which she continued to practice for over five years in three different cities. Diana explores the conservation land around her neighborhood, and when it gets cold and snowy, snowshoes the trails. For other writers it may be bowling, disc golf, in-line skating, yoga...anything that gets the heart pumping and the mind off of writing. Don't fret if your idea of exercise is walking to the fridge to replenish your onion dip; any class, from flower arranging to Chinese, can shake up a writer's life and lead to fresher ideas. Diana, who is an avid knitter, takes classes on online platforms like Craftsy and Creativebug, and practices her rudimentary German with Duolingo, an app on her Android phone.

Mine your life.

For Diana, the creative boot came from starting a family. When she and her husband learned they were expecting a baby, suddenly a whole new market opened up for her: parenting magazines! She pitched stories on new advances in prenatal testing and essays about strangers who were compelled to touch her enormous belly. Then when her son was born, she realized she not only got a beautiful baby boy, but she got a little moneymaker, too. She lugged her six-month-old to a child modeling agency to research a proposal on agency scams, and the drool cascading over his lips became fodder for a *Parenting* magazine piece. Having a baby admitted her into a whole new world—mothers' groups, playgroups, doctors' offices, the highway at 3 a.m. when her son was teething—and gave her a mother lode of great story ideas.

We don't recommend you run out and get yourself or your mate in the family way for the sole purpose of boosting your income, but think about recent major life changes. Are you getting married next year? Think bridal magazines. Did you suffer through a painfully awkward first date last week? How about a funny relationship piece for a men's magazine? Have you changed your diet and exercise habits, lost 50 pounds, and kept the weight off for more than two years? Consider a reported essay on your weight loss journey for a health and fitness magazine.

Take off.

Sometimes you have to empty your mind of all the junk that's bouncing around in there to make room for new, fresh ideas to come in—and what better way than to take a break? Once, Linda was hit with a writer's block the size of Montana; all her ideas were stale and boring. So she cleared a couple of days on her schedule, packed her bags, and headed north to a B&B. Soaking in a hot tub and drinking port in front of a roaring fire certainly helped her forget about writing for a little while, and when she got back to the office, the ideas started flowing again. Now, once or twice per year Linda spends two or three days at a local hotel to get away from it all and relax.

Diana finds it a little harder to take off for B&Bs, but she has other ways to take breaks. When her son was a toddler, Friday night was "Mom's Night Out." She left the little one with Dad, who parked himself in front of The SciFi Channel for the evening while she headed to a local bookshop to chill. After a long week of writing combined with childcare and housework, Diana was brain dead, but a few hours of drinking coffee and flipping through magazines revitalized her. Bonus: that toddler is now a 15-year-old who fondly remembers watching *Star Trek* reruns with his dad.

Taking a break doesn't always require a lot of free time and cash. Even one day of reading on the couch instead of staring frustrated at a computer screen can bring on an infusion of creativity.

Ideas are everywhere—except when they aren't. Don't let the "rule" that you can simply pull ideas out of thin air make you feel frustrated and insecure; instead, when you experience writer's block, try one of our tactics for busting through it.

Never share your ideas with other writers.

Did you ever have a great idea you couldn't bear to write? Say you came up with an idea about how do-it-yourselfers should know when to call in a professional for help—when they don't have the correct tools for a job, for instance, or when a job is too complicated for non-professionals. You know this idea would sell to one of the many homeowners' magazines out there. It's a great idea!

But day after day, that idea grows moldier on your to-do list. Even though you're sure it will sell, you're too busy to bother...or maybe, as great as the idea is, it's not something you're truly interested in researching and writing. Why not pass the idea along to a friend who can cash in on it?

Linda once called Diana to complain that she had nothing good to pitch to her editors. (Everyone goes through writing troughs, even an experienced freelancer like Linda!) Diana had hundreds of great ideas, but no time to get them circulating. She figured, "Why not share them with a friend?" So she whipped out her bulging idea file and passed a bunch of really good ones to Linda. That certainly changed Linda's mood! She took a few of them, and right there on the phone, reslanted them to fit her target publications. The next day she called Diana back and informed her that one of the ideas had sold to *Men's Fitness* for $1,600! Later, she reslanted the idea, pitched it to *Family Circle*, and tallied another $2,500 for the effort.

One of Diana's other writing buddies said, "Holy smokes, you must have been angry that you didn't pitch that story yourself." Actually, she was almost as thrilled as Linda was! The way Diana looks at it, there have been plenty of times Linda has bailed her out of a pit of despair or let Diana use her name with an editor at Magazine X. Diana knows there isn't

80 | LINDA FORMICHELLI & DIANA BURRELL

enough time in the day to write every good story that crosses her path, so until she figures out a way to make 24 hours stretch even longer, it makes perfect sense to pass on what she can't use to someone who can.

Linda has also done her share of sharing. When she realized an assignment with a major woman's mag might be a conflict of interest, she called her editor and urged her to give the job to one of her writer friends—which the editor did.

We urge you to look around at your writing cohorts. Is there someone who could use a little of your help? If so, don't be stingy—offer to give them a few ideas, or brainstorm with them, and don't be surprised if you feel a little better about yourself in the process. Besides, the next time you hit an idea slump, the people you helped in the past may come to your rescue.

RENEGADE RULE-BREAKER

Carol Tice

Carol has been writing professionally for over two decades. Her first freelance gigs in the early 90s were for the *LA Times* and *LA Weekly*, and she went on to write freelance for many business and airline magazines. Carol runs the Make a Living Writing Blog and the Freelance Writers Den, a community of over 1,200 writers that includes free classes, a junk-free job board, forums, and more.

What's the biggest challenge you've faced as a freelance writer, and how did you overcome it?

Probably my insecurity over not having a degree. It really wasn't until after I had worked 12 years as a staffer and won a prestigious national business-writing award that my paper had never previously won in its 25-year history that I went, "You know...maybe they're not going to bust me and kick me out of the club. Maybe I'm *good* at this. And I've learned how to do it. And I'm qualified, and I have a right to be here."

What a lot of wasted time! Our writing *is* our proof that we can tell a story. But basically, I kept building a body of work, until it was irrefutable that I could report a story and tell it in a compelling way.

You started the Freelance Writers Den in 2011, and the site has 1,200 members and a very busy forum. What are the biggest misconceptions you see about freelance writing that are holding new writers back?

It's all between our ears. We have a lot of excuses: "The economy is bad." "I don't know enough." "I'm too young." "I'm too old." "I don't know enough technology." "I don't have any 'connections,' so I can't get gigs." "I'm in a small town, so there are no gigs." "I'm not good enough." "I'm not ready yet." All lies. Stop generating negative scenarios in your head, and start marketing your business!

We also have a lot of assumptions: "Oh, I assumed they would pay me without a contract." "They weren't very clear on what they wanted, so I just went ahead and wrote and hoped it would be okay." "I bid on this website project assuming their pages would be 300 words or so, and it would be maybe 10 pages—but it turned out to be 50 pages that were 1,000 words long."

Don't assume! Ask. Ninety-five percent of the questions you're having about freelance writing can be answered either, "It depends" or "Ask your client or prospect."

What "rules" have you broken so far in your career?

You mean, besides the part where I applied for, got, and held two staff writing jobs as a college dropout, both of which required a B.A. in English or journalism?

I think another big rule I broke was that I built a thriving freelance career after getting fired from my last staff job, after a new editor came on who I totally clashed with. A lot of people implode after they get fired. Their confidence is destroyed, and they spend years staring and collecting unemployment.

Instead, I was like, "Yippee, now I can freelance again!" And within six months, I had replaced my income.

I think there's another rule that freelance writers can only earn so much—and that it will usually be *less* than you earned in your day jobs. A couple years in, I had the insight that my earning potential was actually *unlimited* as a freelancer. I got out of the starvation mentality. And then, everything started to happen—self-publishing, building Freelance Writers Den, and creating a diverse income that is now about eight times more than what I made at the end of my staff writing career!

You've written a lot of books about freelance writing. What new things did you learn about freelance writing as you were working on your books?

What I've learned is, freelancing is a complex business! There's always more to know. And no matter how much detail you explain something in, writers want more.

And often, writers get trapped in a cycle of learning-learning-learning without implementing anything. Learn something, and then go *do* it. Then, learn more.

You've been freelancing for two decades now. How has your writing business changed over the years?

Well, I started out earning $50 for book reviews from an alternative weekly, and most recently I've done a couple of $3,000 articles, one for *Forbes* and one for *Delta Sky*. Over the years, I just kept raising my floor of what I was willing to write for, and aiming higher.

At this point, I'm also heavily diversified with business clients, my 12 ebooks, and teaching. I think any writer working now should be thinking about how they can create passive income through online assets that could keep earning for them. That can be part of a writer's retirement plan!

Do you have any advice for aspiring magazine writers?

Don't be wedded to print. Magazines are moving online, and online article revenue is going up. They're creating more online-exclusive content, and there are high-quality brand journalism projects that look like online magazines, but the client is a business. Just follow the money and your interests.

Also, the world of magazines is incredibly diverse. Don't focus only on major consumer magazines. Tons of industries put out magazines for their customers, like airlines and hospitals. Industry and association trade publications are great markets, too. The other day I was reading a great lifestyle magazine in a therapist's office, and it turned out to be put out by a regional grocery chain!

The world of magazines is definitely in flux, but our desire to read interesting stories and learn things that improve our lives or uplift us isn't going away. Ride the trends and see where the opportunities are.

Nearly every well-paid writer I know also writes for business clients, not just magazine publishers. Think about having a diverse stable of clients, so if one industry or magazine goes down, it's not devastating to your income.

CHAPTER 3

No-Fear Marketing: Now Turn Those Ideas Into Assignments

No part of the freelance writing business is as rife with misconceptions as marketing. Would you believe you can write super-long query letters (sales letters pitching your idea), pitch magazines you've never read, and even cold call editors? Believe it, because it's all true.

BREAK THIS RULE

Be familiar with the magazine before pitching it.

Believe it or not, even this rule can be broken, although editors will probably put a price on our heads for saying so. In fact, Linda's first assignment (for which she was paid $500) was from a magazine she found listed in *Writer's Market*; she had never actually seen the magazine before she queried.

If you don't believe us, maybe you'll believe these writers who sold ideas to magazines they'd never read:

> *My first two writing assignments were from magazines that I had never heard of, let alone read. In fact, the second writing assignment was with a magazine that I couldn't get a copy of even after I had landed the assignment. The first time I read the magazine was when they sent me my complimentary copy after publishing my story in their publication. I think with both of these articles the thing that hooked the editor was that I was offering a completely different view on their topic. I had no preconceived ideas about what should go in the magazine and just queried with what I wanted to write about.*
>
> *—Freelance writer Liz Palmer*

> The Canadian Writer's Journal *carried a market listing for* NeWest Review *that stated the magazine covered politics and entertainment for West Canada. I pitched them a story about housing shortages in British Columbia, but little did I know that they focused solely on the Canadian Prairie provinces. They accepted my query anyway on the condition that I tailor the ar-*

ticle towards people moving from the prairie provinces to BC. It was my first sale!

—Freelance writer James D. Thwaites

I'm almost embarrassed to say that I wrote an article for the official "Babylon Five" magazine having never watched the show or read the mag. It's not something I'd recommend, but it got me a nice paycheck. Basically, I had interviewed an actor named Robin Sachs and during the interview I found out that he had appeared in "Babylon Five" a number of times, so I pitched the interview to the magazine. They wanted it, but they wanted it skewed toward his experiences on the show, of course. At the time I had no idea that the show was full of different kinds of aliens with a variety of agendas. I survived by hitting up my internet friends until I found one who watched the show regularly. He gave me a crash course and the article was a winner!

—Freelance writer Cynthia Boris

I have written for several magazines without ever having seen them, mainly parenting regionals outside of my region, such as Atlanta Baby *and* Minnesota Parent. *As far as I'm concerned— and this could be completely inaccurate—they all seem to be very similar in their content needs. I've also written for a couple of subscription-only e-pubs that I had never seen. In one particular case, I knew the one assistant editor rather well, and she gave me more details about what they wanted than were in the guidelines, so that was very helpful.*

—Freelance writer Lisa Beamer

If you can't find a magazine on the stands or locate its article archives online—a rarity, but it happens—but you've read the guidelines online or its listing in *Writer's Market,* you can sometimes get a pretty good idea of what the editors are looking for. Besides that, if you can't find a magazine on the newsstand, it's probably not a very big publication—and it may be much easier to break into. Editors might not like the idea of a writer pitching a magazine he's never read, but in the competitive world of freelance writing, speed and efficiency are what it's all about. The more you pitch, the more work you get. If you're fairly certain you can turn out a salable idea for a publication even though you can't get your hands on an actual print or virtual copy, why not take the risk?

This rule-breaking tip is meant to keep you from not pitching a pub you love only because you can't get your hands on a copy; if you can find the magazine on the newsstand or online, you really should take a look at it. "A lot of freelancers are lazy," says *Shape*'s former editor-in-chief Anne Russell. "They won't spend $3.99 to do some market research that will help them tailor their pitch." For example, Russell regularly fielded pitches for 3,000-word profiles of professional sportswomen. "It's clear that these writers haven't even looked at our magazine," she says. "We don't do 3,000-word profiles." Considering that a magazine in this league probably gets hundreds of pitches every week, you're probably writing yourself a rejection if you don't check out the magazine thoroughly before sending a pitch.

Buy six back issues
of every magazine you want to pitch.

Here's a paradox: Editors expect writers to read the last six issues of their magazine before pitching—but what magazine writer can afford back issues of every publication she's targeting?

We hear this excuse from so many writers, who don't seem to realize that most magazines have at least some of their articles online, if not entire back issues. Even if a magazine doesn't post every article online, reading through the online archives can give you a good enough idea of the topics they cover, their readers' demographics, and their writing style.

Prefer to read your target markets cover to cover? This is a great way to get to know your target magazines since you can learn a lot from the ads, the editor's letter to readers, the masthead (the list of editors at the front of the magazine), and other non-article parts of the pub; however, you can do that without shelling out a bundle for a pile of pages.

Since the second edition of the book was released, the magazine world has embraced digital technology. Now you can subscribe to magazines through Amazon, Nook (B&N), iTunes, and Google Play, through sites and apps like Texture and Zinio, and even for free through your public library. Many publications go so far as to offer free Android or iPhone apps that let you read their (paid subscription) magazines on your smartphone or tablet. This movement toward providing digital content to readers has been a boon to writers, especially those who live far from a well-stocked newsstand, or who live abroad but do have internet access. Really, the magazine world is your oyster these days!

If you're old school and like to research magazines in their print format, spring for a year's subscription, since that will be cheaper than six newsstand copies. Even better, check bill inserts and membership reward programs for special deals. American Express, for instance, sometimes lets you use membership points to "buy" subscriptions to magazines, and Diana has used these points to subscribe to *Glamour*, *Writer's Digest*, and *Town & Country*. Be aware, however, that renewals may be automatically charged to your credit card. Keep good records!

And if you're too cheap to spring for a magazine subscription, do what Linda did. When she first started freelancing, she stuck a note in her neighbors' mailboxes asking them to drop used magazines on her front porch instead of into the recycling bin. In addition to learning about her neighbors' tastes in reading materials, Linda learned about magazines she never knew existed. She also had a deal with her hairdresser to periodically cart away the piles of magazines that threatened to take over the shop.

Here are some other ways to score magazines on a budget:

Visit your town's recycling center.

Freelancer Sheilagh Casey's town has a trailer dedicated to recycled magazines and slick junk mail.

Look for magazine swaps.

Before relocating, writer Kelly James frequented a library that had a magazine swap. "People could leave magazines they no longer wanted and take whatever ones caught their eye," she says. You can also start a swap with your freelancing friends.

No swap at your local library? "Ask your library to maintain a box for magazine swaps," suggests Freelance writer Claire Jones. "We had this locally, and no one really minded if you mostly took magazines (rather than donated them) as they always had stacks of them. Some really unusual titles as well."

Get up really early on Saturday mornings and haunt yard sales.

Writer Beth Lee Segal relies on tag and garage sales to buy back issues of magazines.

Ask friends, co-workers, and relatives for recent magazines.

When Diana was working full time in an office, she asked co-workers to bring in old magazines from home. She asked specifically for the types of magazines she wanted to write for and received stacks of pubs in return.

Join Freecycle.org.

This free, nonprofit service is a network of over 5,000 groups with more than nine million members around the world. You can post "wanted" ads, and also see "offers" from local members who are looking to offload unwanted items. As Linda was working on this chapter, two Freecycle members in her local group posted offers for stacks of magazines: *Wired*, *Popular Science*, *Travel and Leisure*, *The Economist*, and *Sky and Telescope*. What a sweet haul for a magazine writer looking to research markets!

Work out or get checked out.

Freelancer Iyna Bort Caruso has had good luck browsing trade and consumer magazines at the gym. Or if you're due for teeth cleaning or a cholesterol check, ask your dentist or doctor if you can clean out their waiting rooms.

Sign up for a free trial.

Some magazines entice readers with offers of no-questions-asked free trial subscriptions, which writers like Don Hinkle take advantage of.

Hop aboard planes, trains, and other vehicles.

Writer Arline Zatz swears by airport terminals. "If you go through the main Continental Airlines terminal building at Newark Airport, you'll find at least a dozen magazines with subjects unknown to many—and good outlets for various work," she says. "They're free for the taking."

Browse the bookstore.

Diana and Linda make frequent trips to their local Barnes & Noble to check out what's new on the racks. While, as we mentioned, the newsstand comprises only a small slice of the magazine market, you don't want to ignore it; you'll often find new publications there.

So while we believe that you don't necessarily have to have read a magazine to pitch it, if your excuse is that you don't want to shell out for six back issues of magazines—that excuse is now busted!

Don't send newspaper clips to magazine editors, or online clips to print publications.

Often, you'll hear magazine pros tell newbie writers that if they want to impress an editor at a glossy magazine they shouldn't send newspaper clips, apparently because newspapers are the bastard children of the publishing world. These same writers nix sending your online clips to print mags since, they say, online magazines are not taken as seriously as print ones.

Many writers we know started out writing for newspapers, and they certainly used their newspaper clips when they started pitching magazines. While Diana held a full-time technical writing job, she did countless feature stories for a local chain of newspapers on everything from honeymoon planning to growing lilacs. And guess what? The editor she approached at *Walking* liked the newspaper clips she showed him.

As for online writing not being taken seriously, maybe that was true in 1999, but it's no longer the case when there are so many well-respected online-only publications, and so many writers showing exceptional writing skills on blogs and other online media.

It's not the medium, it's the message—and the message is this: Editors like good writing. If you've written truly wonderful pieces, and they happen to have appeared in your local newspaper or online, few editors are going to turn their nose up at them.

In any case, Linda always says, "You gotta use what you got." If your only clip is from a tiny website or even your college newspaper, that's what you use. When you have scads of samples under your belt, you can worry about matching the clips to the publication you're pitching. Linda used a review of a dialectology text she wrote for the scholarly journal *Language* as a clip when she sent her very first pitch...and it worked!

The "rule" that you need to send the exact right clips to the exact right markets in order to succeed with a pitch does nothing but hold newer writers back. Impress editors with your ideas and your writing, use whatever clips you happen to have to show you're familiar with the publishing process, and you'll be fine.

BREAK THIS RULE

Don't write the full article! First send a pitch, then write the article when you get the assignment.

Normally this rule is a good one. However, Linda's editor at *Writer's Digest* once mentioned that from new writers, he likes to get what he calls an "on-spec" query. This is where you write up your article and then send a compelling pitch that says, "I've already written this article; would you like to take a look?"

The idea of the on-spec query is that it's risk-free for the editor; he doesn't have to offer an untested writer an assignment with a contract and pay, and risk that the writer can't deliver and he'll end up with a hole in the magazine.

The on-spec query might be another good tool in your arsenal of marketing tactics. If you're a new writer and have found that editors aren't willing to take a chance on you, try it and see if it helps you break through that barrier. Then, you'll have experience and clips you can tout in your future queries.

BREAK THIS RULE

Research the magazine and your assignment topic and then start pitching. Why waste your time doing more?

An oft-quoted rule of freelancing is that you need to be as efficient as possible, so you earn as much as you can in the least amount of time. This makes sense—but not if it leads you to cut corners and results in less work.

So yes, you need to research both your market and your idea (though not always; see "BREAK THIS RULE: Be familiar with the magazine before pitching it")—but if you truly want to thrive, the research doesn't end there. Smart freelance writers also research their editors.

Plug your editor's name into a search engine and see what pops up. You may find that the editor went to the same small liberal arts college as you, or has a similar hobby, or once lived in the same town. Sometimes, you can even find things like transcripts of talks they've made to free-lancers in which they specify what kinds of articles they're commissioning.

These are all good icebreakers you can use in your pitch letter. For example, one of Linda's friends found out the editor she was pitching a story to liked a certain author. She sent the editor an essay she had written about that same author, and ended up landing a monthly column in the magazine.

BREAK THIS RULE

Keep your queries short.

We're not going to go in-depth into the art of the query letter in this book, because there's enough advice and information on this complicated topic to fill a book of its own. (In fact, we wrote it! It's called *The Renegade Writer's Query Letters That Rock*.) But we do want to address some common query misconceptions since query letters are a tried-and-true way to land magazine assignments. The first, and probably most prevalent, of those misconceptions is that query letters must be brief.

For her first two years of freelancing, back in the days when you mailed your pitches, Linda sent one-page query letters to top women's markets, as advised by all the writing books and magazines. Then, one day, an editor from *Woman's Day* called and said she preferred to see more research in queries. Within a few months, two- and three-page queries landed Linda assignments with *Redbook*, *Woman's Day* and *Family Circle*.

For her part, Diana landed her first freelance assignment with a two-page, single-spaced snail-mailed query. Even though she, like most professional freelancers, rarely pitches by snail mail these days, her emailed pitches, especially with new-to-her editors, tend to be on the longer side. And freelancer Roxanne Nelson e-mailed a three-page query to *The Atlantic* and received an encouraging response from the editor. As she points out, "With online queries, you can't really see the page breaks!"

Other editors agree that bigger, so to speak, is better. "Since ours is a health magazine, I'd rather see a longer, better-researched query that gives me some indication the writer knows what he or she is talking about," says Denise Foley, former deputy editor of *Prevention*. "Actually, most queries I get reflect a lack of depth and sophistication about health issues."

We're not saying that every query has to rival *War and Peace*. If you've worked with the editor before, a quick outline of your idea may be all that she needs to give you the go-ahead. Diana, for example, emails informal one-paragraph pitches to her editors. And as Linda was working on this chapter, she won a $600 assignment from *Writer's Digest* from a two-sentence pitch. Not a bad return from a query that took a minute to write!

Some editors do prefer shorter pitches. When she was interviewing editors of men's magazines for an article in *The Writer*, Linda found they liked pitches to be as short as possible. "Women tend to be more chatty, so you can write longer queries for women's magazines," one editor said. "Men are more blunt and to the point."

The moral of the story: Tailor the length of your query to your topic and to the type of magazine you're pitching. If you need more words to include all the research and information you think is relevant, go for it. Don't fret; length won't be a deal-breaker if your query rocks. On the other hand, if you have an idea that takes one short and snappy paragraph to explain, then write one paragraph—no more.

BREAK THIS RULE

Pitches are business letters, so keep them professional.

Many of the queries and letters of introduction (LOIs) we see from our students and coaching clients are well-written and boast great content. They offer up impressive credentials, contain stellar ideas, and include everything a pitch needs.

Except personality.

Too often we see writing that's dry and business-like. This is especially common among newer writers, as they overcompensate for their lack of experience by using big words where small ones would suffice, overdoing the passive, and underusing contractions—so they come off as stiff and formal, like a business memo from the local cracker factory.

Think about it: When you read magazines, blogs, and websites, the language is typically conversational, even upbeat. When you write a pitch, you want the editor to be able to envision your writing in her magazine.

Here are some tips for livening up your writing:

1. Use Contractions

We often read credentials paragraphs that say, "I am a writer in Chicago who has written for X, Y, and Z. I am a fast writer and I have won several awards for my writing."

Stiff!

Now try it with contractions: "I'm a writer in Chicago who's written for X, Y, and Z. I'm a fast writer and have won several awards for my writing."

See the difference?

2. Take a Hint from Your Target Market

Read through the archives of the publication you're targeting and lift any words of phrases they use. For example, when Linda pitched *Redbook* with "The Better Orgasm Diet," she noticed they use lots of short, snappy words, so she wrote in one of her tips, "Ditch the caffeine and nix the alcohol." Result = sale! (It was one of Linda's first national sales.)

3. Get Personal

Don't be afraid to put some of yourself into your pitch. For example, if the market you're pitching is your favorite publication and you've been reading it faithfully for the last ten years, you can always mention that in your credentials paragraph. If the topic you're pitching has personal significance to you, let the editor know.

You can also start pitches with personal anecdotes when appropriate. For example, one of Linda's recent students led in with the story of how she has trouble shopping for Mother's Day cards because, well, her mom wasn't as great as the ones described in the cards. What a lede!

4. Make Them Laugh

Are you a funny writer? Unless you're writing about cancer or terrorism, feel free to let it show. For *The Renegade Writer's Query Letters That Rock*, Linda and Diana interviewed one writer, who wrote for *Mental_Floss*, who would start off his pitches with a joke, and another writer—who had cracked some pretty impressive publications himself—ended his successful pitch about a blues singer with, "And if you don't buy my story, I just don't know what I'll do."

In Linda's LOI, she often tells prospects "I'm fast, easy to get along with (no diva here!), and professional." And her email sig line and business card used to say, "My clients think I'm swell." Humor can really help lighten up what could otherwise sound like a desperate sales pitch. It says, "I'm good enough that I'm not afraid to show you who I really am."

5. Talk to a Friend

If you're having trouble losing the formal tone, try rewriting your pitch as if you're talking to a friend. Diana goes so far to draft her queries as an email to her college friend in California. Chances are you wouldn't write to a college friend as if you were writing a memo to your boss's boss about Friday's lunchtime meeting.

In short, forget the "rule" that pitches need to be all business. If you want to make more sales, be yourself.

BREAK THIS RULE

Never email a pitch with attachments.

If you bother to read magazine's writers' guidelines, most of them will invite you to pitch via email with the caveat, "No attachments, please." Some magazines go further and will assure you that emailed pitches with attachments will be discarded upon receipt.

In years past there was good reason for this attachment phobia as it was the most effective way for bad guys to spread their evil computer viruses or sneak their way to remote access a computer system. While viruses and system attacks can still be transmitted or instigated by email attachments, legitimate companies have smartened up by installing aggressive virus protection against these malicious attachments, allowing legitimate attachments through to their intended recipients. On top of this, the evil geniuses who create these viruses, worms, and trojans have moved on to other, more effective ways to transmit their repugnant creations. Of course viruses and other nasty bits are still transmitted by email, but even tech-unsavvy folks are clued in to the email from a stranger that reads, "Open the attachment to claim your million-dollar prize!"

You've probably figured out by now that the vast majority of editors working today are cool receiving writer pitches by email...that is, a pitch that's included in the body of an email message. There's no reason we can think of where you'd want to send your pitch letter as an attachment on an email message. If you wrote your letter in Word (or Google Docs or another word processing package), simply copy and paste it into the body of your email.

Freelancer Carol Alexander, however, proves that breaking the "no attachment" rule can work under the right circumstances. When she was trying to break into magazine writing ten years ago, like many writers she struggled to get an editor's attention with her query letters. She was getting ready to send off another pitch—a home improvement how-to—to a national magazine when she thought, "A picture is worth a thousand words, right?" She attached a photo of her own completed home improvement project to the emailed pitch, hit send, and shocker...the editor not only read her pitch but opened the attachment and gave her an assignment.

Alexander says, "To verify that it was the picture that did it, I recently had reason to unearth that query letter and, just as I feared, it was terrible. I'm convinced that without that photo, I wouldn't have gotten my break into a national publication."

The takeaway? Be smart about using the attachment feature when pitching your ideas. If you've got a very visual story idea—for example, you want to profile a garden designer who recreated Monet's Water Lilies at Giverny in her backyard in Illinois—go ahead and attach a .jpg of the woman's garden. A clear photo of a stunning garden will probably grab an editor's attention faster than the written description of said garden. Or if you've got a travel story where photographs are going to be key, send a couple along with your pitch, especially if the assignment will hinge on the quality of photographs you can provide.

However, if the publication makes it abundantly clear they are dead-set against email attachments, skip sending them with your pitch but do tell the editor you'd be pleased to send photos, or any other files that bolster your pitch, upon request.

If you don't receive a response from an editor, assume she doesn't want your idea and move on.

This "rule" is a reaction to the fear that you'll bug an editor if you follow up on a pitch. But as socks go missing in the laundry, so do pitches get lost in cyberspace. Call or email the editor to find out the status of your pitch if you haven't heard back within a reasonable time period, say two or three weeks...sooner if your idea is time sensitive.

Why bother following up? Linda once sent a pitch to a career magazine and didn't hear back for two months. When she finally called to follow up, the editor told her that he had never received her pitch, but that the publishing group had started a new magazine that would be a perfect home for her story. Success! If Linda had given up on the pitch, she would never have made that sale. She's spoken with other writers who've experienced the same situation.

Eric has also learned not to let his pitches die a quiet death in the hands of editors. Whenever he sent a pitch to *GAMES* he'd get crickets, even though he'd written a dozen pieces for the mag already. He'd wait a week or two and call the editor, and would often end up landing the assignment by phone. Why didn't the editor respond to the pitches if they were good enough to warrant an assignment? We have no idea, but Eric got smart to the editor's modus operandi and scored many dollars.

Here are some potential reasons your pitch has gone unanswered, beyond getting lost in transit:

The staff is too busy.

If you think you have a problem with deadlines, imagine trying to put out an entire publication—every thirty days! The stress of the publishing world can cause major delays, since responding to unsolicited pitches is understandably a low priority task.

The staff is almost nonexistent.

Sometimes there's no one available to review pitches, which means your pitch is sitting in a to-be-answered pile somewhere in an editorial email box. "We're a small association; I don't have an editorial assistant here and don't expect to get one anytime soon," says Cindy Sweeney, former editor of *Dimensions* magazine. "I respond to queries as quickly as I can, but unfortunately I don't have time to make them a priority."

The economy stinks.

A mushy economy means editors are more careful about handing out assignments, which can leave your pitch languishing in a pile of unread submissions. "There's a definite relationship between the speed of acceptance and the overall financial outlook for publishers," says Evan Harvey, former editor of CareerBuilder.com. "You don't want to commit $400 to an article that may be worth $200 in a month."

Your pitch is on file.

Sometimes, an AWOL response spells good news for the writer because it means your pitch is still under consideration. "I have things that have sat in my file for a year or more that I've eventually purchased," says Daniel Kehrer, former editor of *Emerging Business*. "I think there's a lot of material that ultimately falls into that kind of twilight zone at a lot of publications." Linda has definitely had the experience of landing an assignment a year or more after pitching!

BREAK THIS RULE

Check *Writer's Market* for the name of the editor to pitch.

Writer's Market is considered the freelance writer's Bible; it's a directory that lists hundreds of paying markets plus details like how much they pay, what they're looking for, who to pitch, and more.

However, by the time *Writer's Market* hits the shelves, many of the publications they list have already had staff changes. Pick up a copy six months after publication, and you can bet that most editors listed are no longer at that publication or in that same position.

Checking the magazine's masthead (the section in the front that lists the staff) ups the odds of finding the right editor to target, and online publications are more likely to have up-to-date editor information on their websites. However, print magazines are prepared months ahead of time, so their masthead may also be inaccurate. Your best bet: Call the editorial department and ask them to name names.

You can find a magazine's telephone number in its masthead, in *Writer's Market*, or on the publication's website. You may need to call the publishing company's main number and ask to be connected to the magazine's editorial department.

Don't be shy about this! Most likely, when you call you will reach the editorial voicemail. If they have one of those systems where you can dial a staff member by name, dial in the name of the editor you wanted to pitch to make sure she's still there. (You can do this after hours if you don't want to risk having the editor pick up the phone.) If the phone system doesn't offer this option, leave a message asking for the name of the person you should pitch for an article on such-and-such.

Sometimes you'll get a human being on the line. Rarely, you'll reach the actual person you want to pitch. And even more rarely, that editor will ask you to pitch your idea over the phone. You may want to practice pitching your idea in less than 30 seconds so you'll be ready if it does happen. If you're worried about stumbling and fumbling for words, try to put your fears aside. Editors tend to be pretty understanding that writers are better at writing than talking.

Phone calls going nowhere? Check LinkedIn and Twitter, and ask around in writers' forums like the Freelance Writers Den to see if anyone knows the name of the editor who handles the topic you're pitching. Researching is a big part of your job as a freelance writer, so use your sleuthing skills to find the info you need.

BREAK THIS RULE

Query letters are the only way to get an assignment from a magazine.

Query letters are touted by some as the one and only surefire way to land an article assignment. And while queries are powerful marketing tools, they're not the only one in the toolbox—especially if you hate writing them to the point that you find yourself putting them off day after day.

As we've said, freelance writing is a numbers game, meaning the more you pitch, the higher your chances of success. The trick is to find a marketing method that you enjoy enough to want to do it over and over (and over), and to work the heck out of it. Here are some you may like:

Letters of Introduction (LOIs)

Linda has broken into more than two dozen trade magazines and at least 10 custom content companies by sending well-crafted letters of introduction, and Diana snagged a series of assignments from an IT trade pub with a single LOI. What's easy about this form of pitch is that you don't need spend a lot of time researching and fleshing out an idea, so you can write more of them more quickly. LOIs work best for trade magazines and custom publications, but you could always try them with consumer mags; some editors do like being able to skim a few ideas and then ask you to flesh out any she may be interested in.

How you can do it:

1. Introduce yourself in a way that *sincerely* shows you're familiar with the publication.
2. Quickly outline a few ideas you have for the magazine, topping each with a killer headline.
3. Brag on your credentials.
4. Ask for the sale.

Of course, that's the way *we* do it; you may find a format that works better for you, or your LOI style may change depending on the publication. For example, if you have a super-impressive credential that makes you uniquely suited to write for a particular market, you could lead with that.

When you're ready to send your LOI, craft an attention-grabbing email subject line. For example, Eric's subject reads, "Writer for Woman's Day, GAMES, Psychology Today & more." If you don't have a lot of writing credits yet, try a subject line like "Do you need a business [health, kids', etc.] writer?"

Social Media

Yes, you can score freelance writing assignments from social media as long as you don't fall into the trap of socializing and following clickbait links all day. Once Linda got a Twitter follow notice from a regional hospital. She sent a direct message saying, "Hey, I'm a freelance writer who writes on health topics. Do you need any help?" The hospital's Twitter rep sent her note along to their marketing person, who asked Linda for clips. Linda ended up writing several $1/word articles for the hospital's newsletter.

In the meantime, the marketing person sent her name along to the hospital system's web guru, who in turn passed it along to the marketing manager at one of their sister hospitals in Virginia. That marketing manager called Linda with a web writing assignment worth $3,000!

How you can do it:

Instead of spreading yourself thin on everything from Facebook to Instagram, pick one form of social media you enjoy and *work* it. Keep an eye on your follow notices so you'll know if someone in a field you write for starts following you, and be proactive by following potential clients as well. Send prospects a quick note letting them know who you are and asking if you can help them. Write and curate posts that would be of interest to your target market. And of course, be sure to keep your posts clean and professional—but not boring and stilted! (See "BREAK THIS RULE: Pitches are business letters, so keep them professional.")

Blogging

We mentioned blogging earlier in the book as a means to building your clips, but also keep in mind it can be a good way to land writing projects without pitching. This strategy works best if you're totally passionate about your blog (meaning it hasn't been languishing for months), it's particularly well-written, and it deals with a topic that's interesting to magazines. Diana has a hobby blog, Hail Britannia, that covers her interest in British food and culture; throughout the years, she's been approached by editors, content developers, and producers to work on writing and recipe development projects after they'd stopped by her blog.

How you can do it:

It's easy! Start a blog. You can get one up and running for free through Wordpress.com, Wix.com, or Blogger.com; shell out a few bucks for a blog hosting company for space to develop your own blog; or pay for a pre-made blog template and hosting through a company like Squarespace.com.

But then comes the hard part: updating the blog with interesting, well-researched posts that'll attract clients. Our advice is to create an editorial calendar for your posts as far as you can into the future (and hold yourself to that schedule), write your posts with the same professionalism you'd bring to a paid assignment, and learn everything you can about publicizing your blog and attracting readers, some of whom we hope will be paying clients. We'll talk more about blogging later on in this chapter.

Referrals

Word of mouth is a powerful way to land assignments since it leverages relationships. For example, one editor of a custom published magazine loved Linda's work, and shared her info with other editors in the group. Linda ended up writing for four magazines at this company. This has happened at more than one publishing group!

How you can do it:

Do kick-butt work for all your clients. Act like a professional, get your work in on time, and write fabulous articles. After you've gotten to know an editor, ask him to introduce you to other editors in the company or in the industry. When an editor compliments your work, ask if you can use his comments in a testimonial that you can use on your website, post on social media, and include in pitch letters.

Phone Calls

A couple of years ago, Linda was at a friend's house and she noticed he had a copy of a magazine called *Choice Health*, which was published by the friend's health insurance company. The masthead didn't list the editor's email address, but it did have her phone number. So Linda called and left a voicemail introducing herself to the editor and asking her if she hired freelancers. The editor sent Linda an email asking for clips, which she sent.

Five months went by, and Linda forgot all about the magazine. Then, suddenly, the editor emailed with an assignment—at $1 per word. Linda ended up writing a few high-paying articles for her before the magazine ceased publication.

How you can do it:

You may have trouble reaching an editor at a big newsstand magazine by phone, but it's not as difficult with local, trade, and custom pubs. You'll most likely reach the editor's voicemail, so have a short elevator speech ready about who you are. For example, in Linda's voicemail she said, "Hi, Julie. I'm a freelance writer who has written on health topics for magazines like *Health, Women's Health*, and *Redbook*. I saw your magazine and was wondering if you assign articles to freelance writers, and if so, if I might send you some clips. You can call me at X or email me at Y. Thanks so much, and I look forward to hearing from you!" (Think calling editors is a crazy idea? More on the "never call an editor" rule later in this chapter.)

Networking

For some bold writers, in-person networking is a great ay to land gigs. "Everyone says that pitch or query letters are the only first step," says freelancer Craig Grigson III, "but I find that face-to-face works better for me. Everyone wants to see clips or proof in writing, but if I can get face-to-face with someone, I can typically build a relationship quickly and easily. Once I have a relationship started, I begin an email correspondence, which eventually ends in a contract." He says this strategy works well for him when he approaches local businesses in need of a blogger or newsletter writer, but it has also worked with a local magazine.

How you can do it:

If you like the idea of pitching in person, you've got to get yourself in front of the people who will buy your work. This could mean attending writing conferences or trade shows where you'll meet editors, or your city's Chamber of Commerce or a local networking group where you can get to know business owners and other professionals who may need the services of a writer.

Other Magazines

Editors tend to read lots of magazines, and if they like an article you wrote, they may come calling to recruit you into *their* stable of writers. Linda used to write for the (now-defunct) *Cleveland Clinic Magazine*. She once received an email from the editor of a medical school's magazine who saw an article Linda had written in *Cleveland Clinic Magazine*, liked it, and was wondering if Linda could write an article for $1,700. Yes, please!

How you can do it:

This is yet another reason to do your very best work on every writing assignment, no matter how impressive (or unimpressive) the publication or how much (or how little) you're being paid. Editors are probably among your readers, and this is the case even with magazines that aren't on the newsstands. You never know when an editor may be reading your article...and if they're impressed, you could end up with more work!

BREAK THIS RULE

If you want to get assignments, you'll need to be on Twitter, Facebook, Instagram, LinkedIn, Pinterest, and every other form of social media on the internet.

Every marketing guru out there wants to sell you on some secret-special ninja social media trick that will have writing clients battering down your doors. Then we poor writers spend the day hopping from Facebook to LinkedIn to Pinterest and back again, trying to follow this "rule" lest we be seen as the wooly mammoths of the internet, and wonder where all those promised clients are.

Remember, every social media guru has a vested interest in your using their preferred platform; they want you to take their classes, buy their books, and so on, so of course they plug their platform as the one-and-only perfect method for attracting clients. While you certainly *can* land writing assignments through social media if you choose the platform you're best at and focus on that, dividing your attentions among several of them is a recipe for burnout (and no work).

For those of you who dislike social media of all kinds, or who feel too distracted by Twitter, Facebook, and the like to be effective at marketing on them—you don't need to be on social media at all if you don't want to. "But what about staying relevant?" you may ask. "Won't editors think I'm out of touch if I'm not on social media?" We writers fear that if we're not visible on all the social media, the world will rush right by us and we'll be seen as old fogeys without a clue.

But consider this: Linda was on Facebook, Twitter, and LinkedIn for *years*, and while she did score an occasional assignment, she can't think of a single time *the mere fact she was using social media* gave her more cred with editors. One of her friends writes for corporate clients and big-name magazines like *Every Day with Rachael Ray* and she has never been on any kind of social media...ever.

If you think high-quality editors are trolling around the internet and bemoaning your lack of a Facebook page, you're madly overestimating how much time they have. These people barely have time to answer their email, much less wonder if you're using Facebook effectively.

In October 2015, Linda killed all her personal social media accounts. She had 300+ Facebook friends, 500+ LinkedIn connections, and over 6,000 Twitter followers. Only *one* of these close to 7,000 people noticed that Linda had stopped tweeting, posting on Facebook, and updating her LinkedIn profile. If Linda's actual acquaintances and readers didn't notice she had abruptly left social media, do you think an editor would notice if someone he doesn't even know wasn't active on these platforms?

We're all busy. When you're following hundreds of people on social media, it all becomes a blur, and you're not likely to even notice when someone stops posting unless they're power posters and you're a hardcore fan.

We have too much to think and worry about in our freelance writing careers to spend time contemplating whether we're no longer "relevant" because we're not posting links to cat videos. If you simply don't enjoy social media, focus on your core values—your writing skill, your compelling ideas, and your professionalism—and use the marketing techniques that work for *you*.

BREAK THIS RULE

You have to have a blog.

You ask someone with more experience whether you should start a blog to help attract clients and let you use blog posts as clips.

Chances are, the other writer will tell you it's *absolutely, totally imperative* that you have a blog. We even heard one freelance writer tell a poor newbie, "You only have a website? But that's so *static*!"

But in the time between the second and third editions of this book, blogging went from *The Next Big Thing* to *Who Blogs Anymore*? We don't think blogs are dead quite yet, but we don't think every writer out there needs one.

If you hope by starting a blog that editors will notice your sparkling prose and throw assignments at you like confetti, the likelihood of that happening is very slim, especially if your blog inhabits a crowded niche (a mommy blog or fashion blog, for instance) or lacks a strong point of view or narrative vision.

When writers ask Diana if they should start a blog to help move their writing careers along, she asks them, "What would you blog about?" and most of them mumble something along the lines of "Beats me." If that's how you'd answer, we feel your time would be better spent developing story ideas appropriate for paying markets instead of wasting time (and money) developing a blog that you hope will make you popular with editors.

If you start a blog, it needs to be because you already have something you really, really want to say. Something you're so passionate about that you can't hold back. Something that you can envision yourself writing about regularly for the indefinite future. For example, Diana and Linda wrote over 1,000 posts on the Renegade Writer blog between 2006 and 2016! That's the kind of commitment you need to make a blog work. If you don't feel moved to write 1,000 posts on a particular topic, a blog may not be right for you. And that's okay!

Some writing experts tell writers that blogs are an easy clip, but blogging is far from easy. If you start a blog you'll need to keep it updated, because nothing looks sadder to prospective writing clients than a blog that hasn't been updated in six months. Also, what happens when you start getting some real magazine clips and no longer need the blog? Will you let it die a slow, ignominious death? Will all that work be for nothing?

It's much easier to start pitching publications based on your experience—for example, if you have a food-service background you would pitch publications in that industry—or to do a free assignment or two to get the clips.

The good news is that your (static!) website works as a clip. If you have excellent copy on your "about me" page, your "hire me" page, and so on, prospects will be able to see you can write. A good compromise to not having a blog at all is to create an "articles" section where you post pieces when you feel compelled to write them, and make sure they don't have dates or comments so they'll be timeless. That's what Linda now does on her Freelance Writing Success Coaching website.

On the other hand, a blog *can* be a helpful tool for some writers in ways that go beyond serving as clips. In our online teaching and coaching, we've met dozens of writers who want to write about topics that would be extremely difficult to place in mainstream consumer publishing, either because of the topic itself or a perceived lack of writing experience in the writer. We will often suggest to these writers that they start blogging about the subject—first, because they tend to have a lot to say about it, but also because it could lead to other opportunities beyond magazine writing, such as becoming an authority on the subject, which could lead to a book contract if the blog develops a large following. In fact, a book contract is the summit of Mt. Everest for a lot of writers, so if that's the goal and you're totally driven and committed to your subject, developing a strong blog presence could be worth the time.

Another way blogging can help your writing career is that it keeps you writing. Especially when you're starting out as a freelancer, it can feel like the publishing world is against you. Having a place on the internet where you can explore what interests you and write about it without an editor cutting it to pieces can be cathartic. And if you develop an audience for your writing, it's motivating to know that your readers are depending on an update from you once a week or every few days.

Keeping a public blog can be fun and rewarding personally, and occasionally, professionally. But don't feel it's a requirement for freelance writing success; it's not.

BREAK THIS RULE

Never call an editor.

The idea of calling an editor on the phone may fill you with disbelief and dread. Editors are busy! If you call them, you'll annoy them! You're a writer, not a performer!

However, many writers land assignments with some moxie and a phone call. We talked above about how Linda called a health insurance company's custom pub and ended up writing a few $1/word articles for them. Another example is freelance writer Elissa Sonnenberg: When she received a form rejection from a national glossy, she called the editor to try to change his mind. "The point of my calling an editor for whom I aspired to write was to establish a rapport with the guy, to become something more than a name on a letter he could easily reject," she says. "So I asked him why he rejected my idea and made some small talk, until I laughingly told him I thought he made a mistake in rejecting my story idea." The editor laughed, too—and gave her the assignment.

You don't have to wait for a rejection to land in your inbox before calling an editor. Freelance writer Judy Artunian once placed a cold call to the managing editor of *Computerworld* magazine. "I didn't have any particular topics in mind for her. I just wanted to know if she was open to using new freelancers," she says. "I intended to leave a voicemail and follow up with an email, but no dice. She answered the phone." The editor said she didn't need any freelancers at the time, but invited Judy to send clips. A few months later, the editor emailed Judy to say things had changed and she was now open to using new writers. "She asked for a query. I sent one and got an assignment the following week," Judy says.

When Diana was starting out as a writer and still working full time, she noticed that her local chain of weekly newspapers published an endless stream of feature articles written by freelancers. The subjects were usually bridal, parenting, and gardening—the very types of stories Diana wanted to write. So during her lunch break she called the newspaper's main office and asked for the assigning editor. When she got her on the phone, she quickly pushed her credentials and asked for an assignment. And guess what? The editor, who was not at all perturbed about taking a phone call, asked Diana to send over her résumé and clips, then gave her two assignments the next day! Diana eventually became an ongoing feature correspondent for the newspaper. (By the way, newspapers editors tend to be receptive to the quick phone call; one of Diana's editors at *The Boston Globe* actually prefers a call over an email.)

It seems counterintuitive to *call* editors to pitch your *writing* skills, but cold calls do work. Linda once mentored a writer who despised writing query letters, so Linda suggested she pick up the phone and start dialing editors, one after the other. Her client reported back that she started working her way down her call list, and within five minutes she had a conversation with a trade magazine editor who was interested in hiring her. So if you prefer pitching over the phone to other forms of pitching, and have a good phone manner, we say go for it.

You can also use the phone for follow-ups. If you sent a pitch and haven't received a response in a reasonable amount of time, it's perfectly okay to call and ask about the status of your proposal. Call the editor and say something like, "On September 20, I sent you a query for an article called 'Please Hire Me.' I haven't heard back from you, so I'm calling to make sure you received it."

"Writers should absolutely follow up on queries, or on any other correspondence, for that matter," says Matthew Alderton, a former editor at *Imagination Publishing*. "In my experience, editors get so bogged down by their day-to-day activities and deadlines that low-priority business, such as correspondence with writers, often falls off their radar. Followups function as excellent reminders and keep the writer, and his or her query, top-of-mind for the editor." Alderton suggests starting out with an email and then following up with a phone call.

In short, don't worry about all that advice you read that you should never call an editor. If you're smart enough to pick up this book, we're pretty sure you can handle yourself on the phone. Editors are human beings, not rapacious writer-eating fiends. If you're courteous, professional, and quick to the point, they won't hang up on you—we promise. *Shape*'s former editor-in-chief Anne Russell told us about a phone pitch from a writer who had a "hot story" about a championship boogie boarder. "It was totally wrong for us," she says, "but I have to give her credit that she called from Chile."

We know it's scary: Many writers we know even admit to getting sweaty when an editor calls them to offer an assignment! Whether you're afraid of initiating a call or terrified of answering, you need to get over this fear—fast. As freelance writer Jennie Phipps reminds us, "Being a freelance writer means being a salesperson as much as 50 percent of the time. Good salespeople know how to work the phones. Good freelance writers have to learn how to do it, too."

You need to be timely.

Writing experts love telling writers their article ideas need to be timely. But what does that even mean? Like maybe pitching an article about an event the week before it happens? Pitching Christmas-related ideas in December?

Time is relative in the publishing world: Believe it or not, *timely* doesn't mean *right now*. In July, what are all editors vetting during staff meetings? If you said patriotic articles, go to the back of the class. Most magazines work six to nine months ahead, which means they filled their Fourth of July issue by January. When Eric emailed a Valentine's Day idea to his *Woman's Day* editor in September, he was told they were already wrapping up the March issue!

Don't fall into the trap of pitching "timely" ideas, like Halloween stories in October. Instead, buy a wall calendar and set it six to nine months ahead. Come May or June, when you're looking at the calendar, you'll be reminded it's time to start brainstorming for Christmas ideas, and in March you'll see it's not the time for pieces on Easter egg decorating tips, but for articles on how to carve the perfect Jack-o-lantern.

Diana keeps something called a tickler file, a collection of 12 file folders labeled by month. Like most people, she gets her best ideas while in the thick of things. For example, she had to plan a couple of holiday gatherings right after her son was born, which gave her a good story idea for a parenting magazine. She wrote the idea down and stuck it into the folder marked "February." When next February rolled around, she reached in her folder and found this, plus a handful of other holiday-focused ideas she'd saved to pitch to her editors.

Need ideas to stick in your files? National holidays are always a great tie-in. Every month is chock full of holidays you can glean ideas from, such as Organize Your Home Day and National Pet Week. Check out websites such as www.earthcalendar.net for other holidays you probably haven't heard of that can lead to great—and *timely*—article ideas.

Write your query according to "The Formula."

It's been drummed into our heads that every query should include the hook (aka the "lede"), the pitch (aka "nut graf"), the body, the creds, and the close—in that order. And while this format is easy and effective, sometimes "The Formula" gets a little stale.

"I'm not a huge believer in formulas," says Alderton. "I think there is always room for flexibility and creativity. I'm not going to dismiss a query because it's not structured in the traditional format, nor am I going to accept one just because it is. It's about catching my attention and getting me interested in your story idea. The traditional format, beginning with a lede, is designed to do that. But there are, of course, other ways to get my attention. I'm open to them all, so long as you get it."

Why not start your query with a compelling quote from one of your sources? Or brag on your credentials in the first paragraph, especially if you have particularly relevant experience? For example, whenever Diana pitched to technology magazines, the first thing she'd mention is that she's a former technical writer who worked in IT. This set her apart from writers who don't know Java from JavaScript. For a query to a women's magazine, Diana started off by mentioning some of the magazines she's written for because she'd learned that this editor liked to work with experienced writers.

If you were referred to the editor by someone he knows, you'd definitely want to start your pitch with "Sarah Taylor suggested I contact you." And if you've written for the magazine before, you can start off by reminding the editor how well received your article was by readers. For example, when Linda queried *Nation's Business* for an article about business travel, she used this lede:

"My article on micromanagement in the November issue of Nation's Business *seems to have hit a nerve in small business owners: I was interviewed on the topic for the radio show 'Small Business Focus,' gave a talk at a Chamber of Commerce in Philadelphia, and have had several trade magazines ask me to write about micromanagement for their industries. Here's a query for another article I think will have a strong impact among your readers."*

Even though some writing teachers will insist you follow their tried-and-true formula for writing queries, you don't always have to stick to the same-old-same-old. Be creative. Experiment and see what works for you. Editors want to see some personality in your writing, not your skill at filling in templates.

Linda sees this template mentality all too often. Some students copy her standard letter of introduction almost word for word as if, because Linda is a writing pro, her way is the only way. One male writer even left in her "no diva here!" line. Please, ditch this rule as fast as you can.

BREAK THIS RULE

Send your pitch to the editor.

Check out the mastheads from any two different magazines, online or off. Managing editor, assistant managing editor, online editor, associate editor, deputy editor, community editor, senior editor...you can go bonkers trying to figure out who does what. "The editor"? *Which* editor?

Even worse, editors make it hard on you by having wildly varying job duties. Several years ago Linda pitched an article to *Writer's Digest* magazine where she would decipher these titles for readers, and they (rightly) turned it down because no two editors at different publications seem to do the same thing. For example, at some trades Linda has written for, the managing editor is the assigning editor. At other magazines, the managing editor handles production, not copy. At a very small magazine the editor-in-chief might be the one to pitch, but at a national magazine with 50 editors you'd be crazy to direct your pitch to the EIC.

So how can you figure out who to pitch at each publication if it's not simply the editor or the editor-in-chief? Here are some tips:

Pick up the phone.

We know we sound like a broken record: "Pick up the phone! Pick up the phone!" But really, if you don't know something the best way to find out is to ask. Call the editorial department at the magazine and ask the assistant, "Who handles the *Your Health* department?" or "Who should I pitch an article about finances to?" Many writers are pleasantly surprised that they get a quick answer.

Go for the obvious.

Some editors have titles that would make them an obvious pick. For example, if you're writing a fitness pitch and there's a fitness editor, there you go! Other magazines will have food editors, lifestyle editors, beauty editors, business editors, travel editors, and so on.

Ask around.

If you belong to a writers' forum or email group, or have a lot of writer friends on Facebook or Twitter, ask there. A kind colleague may be willing to share that info. Be sure to supply your email address on the forum or invite Direct Messages so respondents won't have to share the info with the whole group.

Don't go too high up the masthead.

If you're pitching a small magazine with only a few editors, you can probably go ahead and pitch the editor or editor-in-chief. But at a large magazine with an extensive masthead, look further down the page to the features editors, department editors, senior editors, and associate editors.

Nix the contributing editor.

A contributing editor is *usually* a writer who writes regularly for the magazine—so she's not really an editor at all. For example, for a long time Linda was listed as a contributing editor on *Writer's Digest*'s masthead, but she certainly didn't take pitches or assign articles. Ditto for Diana, who was listed as a contributing editor at a fitness magazine and a food magazine merely because she wrote regularly for them.

Forget the copy editor, too.

This is also not an assigning editor.

When in doubt, go for a senior editor.

If you called and received no response and none of your writer friends were able to help you, we often find that pitching any senior editor is a safe bet. If that editor isn't the right one, she'll likely send your pitch along to the correct editor.

BREAK THIS RULE

Sell the article idea and then interview your sources.

Believe it or not, many professional magazine writers interview sources *before* they even get the assignment. Compelling quotes not only give your pitch some zip—they also show an editor you know how to find good sources and get good quotes.

The problem is this: How do you convince expert sources to give you the time of day when you don't have an assignment in hand—that is, when you can't guarantee them a media placement?

Many experts (especially experts who bill themselves as media-friendly sources, such organizations' spokespeople, and as those listed on media services like ProfNet) understand that writers need a few good quotes to convince editors to give them an assignment, and they're generally happy to oblige. When you call or email these experts, let them know which magazine you're pitching and stress that you'll need only a few minutes of their time. (If you're pitching several magazines simultaneously, mention the most impressive one from your list.) For example, here's the email Linda usually sends to prospective sources:

> *Dear Natalie:*
>
> *I'm working on a proposal for* Family Circle *magazine about how to save money without feeling the pinch. I see from your bio that you're an expert in this subject. Would you be available to talk for a few minutes via email or phone so I can get some good quotes for my pitch? If I get the assignment, I'll let you know and we can arrange a date and time for a more in-depth interview.*

Thanks, and I look forward to your reply!

Diana used to write a lot of articles that quoted parents of young children, so with these queries, she included two or three "real people" quotes to show her editors the topic was truly something on parents' minds. Sometimes it's easier to get "people on the street" than experts because you can turn to your social media network for anecdotes and quotes.

You don't necessarily *have* to talk with sources before writing up your query, but doing so will make your pitch that much stronger. Even better, once you land the assignment—which you'll have a better chance at doing if you show you're a good researcher and interviewer—some of your work will already be done.

All this may seem like a lot of work for a query you're not even sure will land an assignment, but as you gain more experience, each step will take less time. You'll have a file of editors you like to pitch to as well as a file of sources who are willing to talk. You'll be able to whip out a query, and more of your ideas will be accepted.

We understand this "rule" is all about efficiency, but while writing a query without talking to experts or "real people" sources is more *efficient*, it's often not as *effective*. For each pitch you're working on, use your judgment to decide whether this rule is one worth following.

BREAK THIS RULE

Always email your pitches.

It's too funny: In the first edition of this book, the "rule" we broke was "Don't email your pitch unless you've already worked with the editor." Way back then, emailed pitches were looked down upon in the writing books and magazines. But today, emailed pitches are expected and nearly every freelance writer shoots their pitches off via email. We hope this book had something to do with this momentous change that's made life easier for writers everywhere!

Snail mail used to be a barrier to entry that kept out the less-than-serious: You had to be pretty dedicated to print out pitches, photocopy clips, stuff it all into envelopes, weigh the packages, buy and affix stamps, and go out to the mailbox or post office to mail your packages. The bad news is that the ubiquitous acceptance of email pitches has resulted in editors being deluged with ideas from all over the world, from writers serious and not-so-serious, because email makes it so easy to zap off ideas in an instant.

If you want to stand out among this veritable flood of pitches assaulting editors' inboxes, you may want to turn back time and try snail mailing your pitches once again. Why not? If you're serious about writing for magazines, show it with a beautiful pitch package. Heck, you could even try mailing nice pitch packages to online magazines and see what happens; it's no more crazy than calling editors to pitch articles, which, as we showed earlier, is a very effective marketing tactic.

The point here is, when everyone and his brother thinks they can write for money, you need some way of standing out as a true professional. And just because everyone is doing something one way doesn't mean you have to do it, too. Experiment with new ideas—even counterintuitive ones—and see if they help you make sales.

BREAK THIS RULE

Simultaneous pitching is strictly verboten.

If you follow some of the advice circulating out there, you'll be pitching your idea to one market, waiting up to 12 weeks (or longer) for a response—by which time your idea is probably out of date—and then pitching it to the next market on your list. Meanwhile, your rent payment is late because you're not making any sales.

Here's our take: If magazine editors can't report back in a decent amount of time (or at all), then they'll have to accept that in order to buy groceries and pay the electric company, writers must email simultaneous submissions.

When Linda was starting out, she'd mail merge her queries with the contact information from up to 15 magazines on her database program. She'd examine the resulting letters on her monitor to make sure the merge worked and to personalize the letters as needed. She'd then set up an assembly line of letters, clips, envelopes, self-addressed stamped envelopes, and stamps, put together the packages, and drop them in the mail. Linda sold a good number of her queries this way.

These days you can do pretty much the same thing, with the advantage that you can pitch via email, saving time and money. Freelance travel writer Roy Stevenson claims the reason he's published so prolifically is because he sends a pitch to every magazine where he thinks his story could fit. In his words: "My distribution lists range from five to 50 magazines, and I sell 90 percent of the stories I pitch. Most freelancers consider themselves lucky if they sell 25 percent to 40 percent of the stories they pitch."

Many editors flatter themselves that their publication is totally different from their competitors'. It's true that competing publications may differ slightly in style and content, but in general an idea that would work for one women's fitness magazine could work for other women's fitness magazines with some minor tweaks.

Of course, we're not advising you to write generic pitches and spam dozens of editors; you should absolutely add customized details to your pitches. You'll need to change the editors' names, the names of the departments you're pitching to, and so on. We suggest keeping a checklist at hand with specific details about each publication so that you don't overlook anything before you click send.

But wait...what if you pitch several publications at the same time and two of them accept your pitch at once? It makes Linda and Diana chuckle when their coaching clients and students wring their hands over this worry, because they spent the previous 30 minutes (or 300 words) agonizing that they'll *never* get an assignment.

While having two editors want your idea at the same time is unlikely, when it does happen, invariably the editor of the second mag curses herself out for being too slow to respond rather than cursing the writer for sending the same idea to multiple publications. If your idea is so great that two editors come knocking on your door, accept the assignment from the better magazine and suggest a different topic twist to the other title. This recently happened with one of Diana's students who was pitching a travel article to newspapers; each newspaper in non-competing markets took different slants with no one the wiser. You can also offer different rights to each magazine—for example, if you're dealing with two non-competing regional publications, you can offer region-specific rights to each magazine. Or you could offer print-only rights to one publication and online-only to another, non-competing pub.

Another tactic is to first send your pitch to all the top-tier markets on your A-list, and if none of them bite, move on to all the markets on your B-list, and so on. That way you don't need to fear that you'll accept an assignment from a local, low-paying sports pub and get a call a week later from *Sports Illustrated* that they'd like your article.

Still afraid the gods watching over Madison Avenue will smite you in your sleep if you send out simultaneous pitches? Then try slanting the same idea for different types of publications instead. For example, Linda sent a pitch about "How Your Lifestyle Affects Your Dog" to dog magazines, then turned around and sent "How Your Lifestyle Affects Your Cat" to cat mags, one of which accepted the idea. She later sold "How Your Lifestyle Affects Your Pet" to a big-name health magazine. That way, if two publications accept the pitch, you can take on both assignments, being careful to write a 100 percent different piece for each one.

We always recommend simultaneous pitching when you don't have a personal connection with the editors—freelance writing is a numbers game, especially at the beginning! However, once you have a few editors you've built relationships with, you'll probably want to give these editors an exclusive on your idea before sending it out to the industry at large. For example, if Linda had a great idea for a health article, she'd send it to her favorite editor at *Redbook* and wait for her response before sending it on to other magazines. Why? First, out of loyalty to an editor who had given her work in the past. Second, she'd get a faster response from *Redbook* since she's a known quantity to the editor.

Brainstorm ideas to pitch to editors.

It's true that good ideas presented well will often result in assignments, which is why many experts will tell you to spend a good portion of your life on the lookout for article ideas. They suggest holding brainstorming sessions, reading widely, and eavesdropping on conversations to find those pitchable nuggets.

Yes, these are wonderfully effective ways to generate salable ideas, but they all require you to brainstorm in a vacuum. Instead of *guessing* at what an editor will like, why not *ask* him what he's looking for and pitch away? They won't always respond, but sometimes they will—and their suggestions will help you better target your ideas and pitch faster.

For example, Diana once had lunch with two of her editors at sister technical publications, and they spent a half hour talking about all the stories they should do in the future. Diana listened and took copious notes for later pitching. Linda asked her editor at *Woman's Day* what she was looking for and received a list of ideas via email. Editors will sometimes also use this opportunity to tell you about changes in the magazine such as new sections you can target.

This works mostly with editors you've written for before; editors don't have time to give hot tips and insider information to every writer who wants to break in. "More established writers, and those I've worked with, will email or call me to talk about what subjects we're interested in," says Denise Foley, formerly of *Prevention*. "I don't return phone calls from people I don't know—I'm not being rude, I just don't have the time." But if there's a magazine you'd like to write for and you'd like some tips on what their needs are, it never hurts to ask!

If you've got an especially supportive networking group, you can also ask your peers to share this kind of information. Once Linda received an email from one of her editors at a women's magazine who was desperate for story ideas in certain areas. Linda passed this information on to several writers in her network, who were then able to tailor pitches based on this editor's needs.

Another alternative to incessant brainstorming: Sometimes the editor's letter in the front of a magazine will give you clues as to what they're looking for in the future. You may find that they've introduced a new section of the magazine or they're going in a new direction with their focus. A careful reader/writer will pick up on these clues and pitch accordingly.

Putting a deadline in your pitch will ensure a faster response.

You may have heard that in order to get a faster response to your pitch, you should include something like, "If I don't hear back from you by X date, I'll assume you're not interested and will send my idea to someone else."

Good luck with that approach! The reason it can take so long to get a response is not because the editor is carefully contemplating your pitch for two months—it's because your pitch is sitting underneath a virtual pile of hundreds of other proposals from other writers. Your deadline could come and go without an editor ever having set eyes on your pitch—and when she finally does get to it, she may toss it in the bin because that deadline you set is long past.

Also, if you're including a deadline in your pitches, we assume that's because you're sending to one publication at a time. Don't forget what we discussed earlier in this chapter: If you hope to make a living as a writer, since so many editors take forever to respond or don't respond at all you'll probably need to submit your pitches to more than one market at a time.

At the same time, though you want to spread your pitches far and wide, you don't necessarily want to announce this to editors; even though they may be in the habit of ignoring pitches they're not interested in, they enjoy the delusion that you carefully crafted your pitch for their eyes and their eyes only. Your deadline may give the editor the idea that you're dying to circulate the query to other pubs, which isn't something they need to know.

"A deadline would tell me the writer was going to offer it to my competition, which would mean that he and we are likely to soon part," says

Brian Alm, former editor of *Rental Management Magazine*. "I'm selfish with the few writers I use. I spend a lot of time teaching them about the industry and working over story plans with them. I don't expect to see them take all that knowledge and grooming to the other magazines in the industry and have their byline show up there after I have made them known in this industry."

Now, if you have a time-sensitive idea that will go stale quickly—for example you landed an in-person exclusive with a well-known actor and she'll be in town next week—feel free to write something like, "Because this is a timely topic, if I don't hear from you by X date, I'll assume you're not interested in the story." Then, follow up a couple days later with a phone call. In fact, if the story is that hot, call, then pitch by email if the editor is interested.

BREAK THIS RULE

Tell the editor how long it will take to write the article.

Many books and articles on pitching suggest that you put in your proposal, "I can have 'My Great Article' finished in three weeks." We guess the writer's underlying assumption is that the editor is going to say something like, "Wow, three weeks! The idea is only adequate, but that delivery date can't be beat. I'll take it!" Unlikely. And what if the editors at this magazine like to have their articles in two-and-a-half weeks, or they prefer to give writers two months to ensure well-researched pieces?

When you land an assignment, the editor will tell you what the deadline is. "For me, it's not necessary for the writer to say how soon they can have the article to us," says John Stark, former deputy editor of *Body + Soul* magazine. "In some cases it sounds as if the writer is a machine who can churn out a generic article in X amount of time. Because we plan our editorial calendar so far ahead, a writer usually has plenty of time to do a story."

By stating a finish date, you may be pulling yourself out of the game before it starts. "It's not a make-or-break issue normally, but it could be," says Alm. "If the writer has no background in my industry and claims he can produce 1,000 words in three weeks on an esoteric or difficult topic that is very industry-specific, I know he's blowing smoke and doesn't know himself well enough to trust."

Make sure your pitch is perfect before sending it out.

No, we're not saying you should skip the spell check. Your pitches should be as pristine as possible, your writing sparkling, and your quotes and stats interesting and accurate. But so many writing books, magazines, and experts hammer in the idea that your pitches need to be 100 percent perfect that writers get hung up on the picayune details of their proposals—which either takes the juice out of their writing or prevents them from sending their work out at all.

Perfectionism is deadly and we think it kills more beginning writing careers than grammar accidents and etiquette gaffes combined. Diana almost fell victim to this problem, but through self-help and experience, she's eradicated perfectionism from her writing life. She studied other, more successful, freelancers and watched how they worked. They didn't fret for days over a pitch; they did the best they could and got the work out there. Diana began keeping a file of all the wonderful things her editors said to her about her writing and her work habits, and whenever she began to feel paralyzed by the need to be perfect, she'd take those notes out and reread them. She also keeps a checklist handy and uses it before sending a pitch out to ensure she's using the right editor name, department title, and so on.

The best cure, however, is to get on with it. No obsessing, no worrying. Write the thing, let it rest, proof it, and hit the "Send" button or pop the query in the mail.

Shape's former EIC Anne Russell understands that even the best writers make mistakes, and this usually comes about because the writer is trying too hard. She, in fact, has done it herself with her own correspondence. "I'll run back to grab the letter from the outbox, convinced that I've misspelled a person's name," she says. "Your brain starts playing tricks on you." Her solution? Let the pitch sit for a day, and when you come back to it, the errors will glare at you. "It's like buying a gun. There should be a waiting period before you send your queries out," she says.

Even if after all your efforts a mistake does rear its ugly head in your pitch, it doesn't have to be a deal-breaker. Both Diana and Linda have sold to major newsstand magazines with pitches that were *missing words in the first sentences.* And once Linda sent a query for Magazine X to an editor at Magazine Y. The query was rejected, but Linda also got a very nice note from the editor assuring her that such mistakes are common and forgivable. Even more encouraging is the fact that with editors getting so much email these days, rarely will they remember that you were the writer who misspelled Mississippi in your pitch!

Many times we've seen panicked posts from writers on forums who wonder whether they should call editors to fess up to mistakes in their pitch. We say, "Don't!" Three-quarters of the time, an editor isn't going to notice a missing word or a typo, especially if the rest of the letter shines. And even if they do notice it, most editors will forgive a minor editorial transgression. Calling attention to it makes you appear insecure and perfectionistic. Consider it a learning experience, hope the editor doesn't notice, and move on to your next pitch.

On the other hand, Russell is not so forgiving of major mistakes. She finds it offensive when a writer misspells her name ("I have a very simple name") and woe to the writer who sends a pitch to the magazine's subscription processing center ("It happens more than you would imagine.") When she was an editor at *Working Woman*, Russell read a query that concluded, "I know dentists will love this article." Clearly, the writer of this gem sent out pitches willy nilly, hoping for any old bite. All these things are deal-breakers for her—and many other editors, too—so if you've made this kind of mistake, don't bother apologizing. In Russell's words, "You've blown it." Don't obsess over it, but move on, knowing there are plenty of other markets out there for you to try.

BREAK THIS RULE

Your #1 goal is to sell the idea you're pitching.

We get questions like these all the time from coaching clients and students:

- How much should I research a magazine before I know it's a good market for my idea? Right now it's taking me hours.
- I want to pitch this publication, but I can't find their writers' guidelines so I don't know if they use freelancers.
- I researched this magazine to see if my idea is a good fit, but they don't have a good department for it/they've never run anything like it/Mercury is in retrograde—so I think I won't pitch them.

These fearful questions all stem from the common, but incorrect, thought that you have one chance to sell an editor, and if your pitch isn't spot on, you've lost out forever. This "rule" keeps writers from pitching their ideas to editors.

But guess what? The goal of a pitch is not necessarily to get an assignment. *The goal of a pitch is to start building a relationship with a client.*

Of *course* you would like to get an assignment straight off, but what often happens is that your pitch doesn't quite make the cut—say, the publication already has a similar article in the works—but the editor is so impressed by your pitch that she invites you to pitch again, or even assigns you a different article.

If you hold off on pitching because you're not fully, absolutely, 100% sure your ideas are a good match, then you're missing out on the opportunity to start a conversation with an editor who may want to hire you down the road.

Your pitch shows what you can do. It shows you have great ideas, can write well, and are professional. Even if it's not a perfect match, it can lead to assignments. Diana even has a letter she's nicknamed "The Little Black Dress Pitch." She has never sold the idea in it to a woman's magazine, but any time she's sent this pitch out, it's resulted in the editor assigning her their own ideas or initiating a new business relationship.

Even more encouragement: Brian Alm, formerly of *Rental Management*, has rejected pitches but given the writers of these pitches assignments from his own pile of ideas based on the writers' obvious talent. "And a number of times I have taken the query and revised the assignment the writer had proposed into something specific to our industry, with quotes and industry interviews and examples, and paid the writer twice what he had originally asked for in order to have this exclusivity," says Alm. Denise Foley, formerly of *Prevention*, has also invited writers of rejected pitches into her stable. "Absolutely! Several of our regular freelancers came to us that way," she says.

The rule that the purpose of a pitch is to get an assignment is perpetuated by self-proclaimed writing experts who aren't able to see the long view. Don't fall for it!

BREAK THIS RULE

Never send the same idea to the same magazine twice.

Ask in a writers' forum if it's okay for you to send the same idea to a publication twice and the chorus will be, "No way! They'll catch on and will blacklist you." But luckily, you're a renegade and are willing to closely examine even the most revered rules.

Like this: Linda once submitted an idea to the editor-in-chief of a writing magazine, who rejected it. A few years later, Linda sent the same pitch to an editor lower on the masthead—and he accepted it!

Another example: One of Diana's editors asked her to write up a proposal about a parenting topic they'd discussed over lunch; unfortunately, the editor's boss shot it down, so the idea was nixed. When Diana met her assigning editor for another lunch in February, she mentioned how much she had wanted to write this article. After some thought, her editor said, "It was a great idea. Why not add [this] and [this] to the proposal, and we'll send it through again?" This time, Diana scored a $3,000 assignment. What may have made the difference? Diana had done a few more features with this magazine, so the editorial regime had more confidence in her ability to tackle a tricky topic. (Diana later learned that the resulting article ended up being one of the most popular articles among the magazine's readers that year!)

Magazines change, editors change, needs change—hey, writers change! Maybe your idea wasn't timely enough when you originally sent it, but some news hook has come up that makes now the perfect time for your story. Maybe the magazine didn't have a health department back then, but now they do. Maybe a new editor-in-chief came in and reorganized the magazine to include more FOBs. Or maybe your editor didn't think you had the chops to tackle the topic when you first pitched it, but now you do.

If your target magazine suddenly looks like a much better market for your idea than it was when you first sent it, don't be afraid to resubmit. You can even write in your pitch, "I submitted this idea to you last year, but see that you've revamped *Eraser Manufacturer's Quarterly* and are running more articles on eraser collecting. My profile of a collector of Disney-themed erasers looks like a good fit, and I thought I'd resubmit it for your consideration." The editor will likely be impressed that you read the magazine so thoroughly and understand her needs.

Also, if a new editor-in-chief came in and shook up your target magazine, you can resubmit your idea to the new editorial team with no qualms. For example, maybe that edgy health idea that *Men's Fitness* rejected a year ago would be a hit with the new editors of the revamped, *Maxim*-ized *Men's Fitness*.

A rejection is a rejection—except when it comes to magazines. In the publishing world, "no" often means "not now."

RENEGADE RULE-BREAKER

Jennifer Lawler

Jennifer Lawler is a writer, a book development editor, and the author of *Dojo Wisdom for Writers*.

How did you get started as a writer?

I've always wanted to be a writer, and when I was in graduate school I did some academic writing that was published. Of course, I wasn't paid anything but it made me believe I could get published. So I started sending out some queries and I ended up doing contract work for McGraw-Hill—working for their textbook department researching. When they felt I could write small sidebars, etc., then I moved up to that, eventually writing teachers' guides and art history textbook chapters.

At the time, I thought I'd be a university professor and write on the side, so I wasn't too concerned about bylines or pay. I was focused just on breaking in.

But when I earned my black belt in Tae Kwon Do, I realized that I could do practically anything I set my mind to. So if I wanted to be a writer, why didn't I go be a writer? I thought for about ten minutes, then chucked the teaching job and started sending out queries. I decided I wanted to be a full-time freelancer and I wanted to write books and magazine articles, and nothing was going to stop me.

So I started writing about things that interested me and eventually published a lot of books about the martial arts (among other things) and the martial arts-related writing really took off. When I reached the point where I had said pretty much all I wanted to say about martial arts, I focused my attention on fiction (and published a number of novels under various pen names) and ghosting and co-authoring nonfiction books where I was the writer and other people were the experts. To me, success has come over the long term because I'm open to the opportunities that arise and recognize that change is constant.

What rules did you break as you broke into books? Into magazines?

I broke the "you need an agent" rule. The first four agents I had were worthless, so I repped myself for sixteen books. Not a big deal. Then an agent found me—I really had no intention of going the agent route again—and she sold a number of my books for good advances. But she "found" me because I was already an established martial arts book author, which wouldn't have been the case if I had thought I needed an agent to get started.

For magazines, I broke the "don't start at the top" rule. With some encouragement from Linda F., I submitted an essay to *Family Circle* and they snapped it up, even though my clips included such national titles as

Martial Arts and Combat Sports and *Inside Karate and Kung Fu*. After that, it was easy to get other assignments from *Family Circle* and others.

I also *always* break the no multiple submissions rule and have all my writing career (I'm referring to book publishing here—for magazine writing, I found that targeting pitches to specific publications netted me a very high success rate versus trying to get assignments from generic pitches). In book publishing, agents and editors rarely respond in a timely fashion, and it might be different if they did, but some of these people never respond or take months to do so—once I got a rejection something like 18 months after I sent three sample chapters to the agent. He didn't really think I was giving him an exclusive all that time, did he? Get a grip.

What's Dojo Wisdom for Writers all about?

Dojo Wisdom for Writers is an inspirational, motivational, and practical book for writers. It contains 100 essential lessons from the martial arts that I (and other writers) have used to build our careers—and which will help writers everywhere. The book contains anecdotes, advice, and exercises for beginning and established writers. It was eye opening to write—hearing from so many accomplished writers who had been down the same path I had. The second edition was recently published, so the information is all updated.

What's the biggest rule you think writers should break, and why?

Break the "I'm a writer so I must be poor" rule. That's the one I hate most. People simply don't believe you can make a living as a writer. If you start out thinking, "I'll never make any money," then you won't. I have always made more than enough money to keep a roof over my head, take amazing trips now and then, and to provide my daughter everything she needs to blossom into an amazing young woman.

It's been ten years since you spoke to us. How has your career changed?

In the years since *The Renegade Writer* was first published, book publishing, like magazine publishing, got turned on its head. The economic downturn that started at the end of 2007 shook everything up. The people who were wedded to doing the same things they had always done faced significantly lower advances, faltering book sales, the rise of readers' expectations that even books should be free, and so on. Ironically, I ended up moving to the editorial side right around that time because that was where the opportunities—for me, anyway—happened to show themselves. My work as a coauthor/ghost turned out to be very valuable to publishers who were looking to outsource their book development work. Staffs were cut but the work still needed to be done and I proved capable of doing it.

After focusing on nonfiction book development for a few years, I became an acquisitions editor for a fiction imprint. After I had done that for a while, I moved back to development work (which I like better than administration/management) and eventually began to teach book development classes for the Editorial Freelancers Association. In the classes, I work with motivated professionals who are committed to improving their skills, and I learn as much as they do. Now I do development work for book packagers and publishers, I teach book development classes, and I still work on my fiction. I'm as in love with my career now as I was twenty years ago, although it looks very different now.

Looking back over my career, I'd say that persistence pays but you have to be willing to change. The people who think they can be the same freelancer they were ten years ago, writing the same things in the same way for the same markets, are struggling to keep their heads above water, whereas those who have been willing to learn and grow their skills to keep up with the new world are succeeding.

CHAPTER 4

Signing on the Dotted Line: Renegades Get Fatter, Fairer, Safer Contracts

Many contracts are bad for the writer: They ask for all the rights to the articles you've sweated over, put you in the hot seat should someone sue the magazine, and give the magazine the right to pay you a fraction of what you're owed if the editors change their minds about your article for any reason. Here's how you can be a Renegade Writer—and make contracts work for *you*.

BREAK THIS RULE

Assume the contract is set in stone.

In a buyer's market the buyer gets to set the terms, and the magazine industry is almost always a buyer's market. That means writers rarely sit in the catbird seat. Many editors automatically hand writers the contract their lawyers wrote up for them—and most writers resignedly sign that contract, so editors aren't exactly compelled to make it more writer-friendly.

If, however, the writer has the temerity to ask for changes, the editor may be happy to make them. Although the publisher has more leverage than writers when it comes to contracts, that doesn't mean you have to roll over and let their lawyers walk all over you. Here are some of the clauses you might want to ask to change:

All Rights/Work for Hire

Many publications these days automatically ask for all rights (aka "work for hire"), where they own all the rights to your work in all media forever, and refuse to negotiate. However, it doesn't hurt to ask. If you think the article has reprint value, tell your editor you'd be willing to sell First North American Serial Rights, where the magazine gets to be the first to print the article in North America. If that's a no go, you may be able to get the editor to agree to "non-exclusive rights," which allows the magazine to reprint the article in its sister publications or sell it to a content provider, but still gives you the right to sell it to other magazines.

Payment

If an editor says she pays ten dollars for a thousand-word assignment, you are not going to talk her up to a dollar a word. But if the rate is a little below what you were expecting, or your minimum rate, it's fine to ask if the editor can bump up your pay.

Don't only ask, though—provide compelling reasons for your request. For example, you might say, "This is a research-intensive project...it will require eight interviews plus some additional footwork. I normally earn about 50 cents per word minimum for assignments like this. I'd love to write this for you, so is there any way you can up the rate a little?" Be prepared for the editor's refusal to budge, and know up-front whether you're willing to walk away or if you'll settle for a lower rate.

You can also angle for extra money if the magazine insists on electronic rights along with print rights. For publication on a website, the National Writers Union suggests a pay level commensurate with first print rights. For other electronic rights, the NWU suggests between 30 and 50 percent of the first print rights fee for use of the writer's work in a single electronic outlet.

Indemnity Clause

Another clause to change is the one where the writer guarantees that the article breaks no laws anywhere in the known universe. The clause goes something like this:

> *Author represents and warrants that any article Author may present under this Agreement shall be Author's wholly original work, not previously published in any media, in whole or in part; that the work will not infringe any person's or entity's copyright, trademarks, service marks, or other proprietary rights, and will not constitute defamation, invasion of the rights of privacy, or infringement of any other rights of any kind of any third party. In the event that any threat, demand, claim, or action is asserted against Magazine X or any of its affiliates, or their officers, directors, or employees, by any person or entity alleging copyright, trademark, or service mark infringement; unfair competition; misuse of proprietary ideas or expression; defamation; invasion of privacy; or any other claim arising out of Magazine X's publication of Author's article, Author shall defend, indemnify and hold harmless Magazine X, its affiliates, and their officers, directors, and employees from any and all liabilities, expenses, costs, damages, settlements, or judgments, including attorney fees, incurred in*

*connection with such threat, demand, claim or action if Author is
shown to have violated his agreements as judged in a court of law.*

How are you supposed to know if you're infringing on the trademark
of some obscure business in Botswana? Ask that this onerous clause be
removed, or at a minimum insist that the phrase "to the best of the author's knowledge," be added, as in, "The author warrants that to the best
of their knowledge any article Author may present under this agreement..."

Deadline

Before you agree to a deadline, make sure it fits into your schedule. If
you have several assignments all stacked up around the same time, or
you're planning a vacation around the proposed deadline time, it's likely
you'll find yourself in a time crunch. Also, you know how long an article
typically takes you to research and write, and you want to give yourself
plenty of leeway in case you run into any snags.

Don't worry about losing an assignment if you ask to change the deadline—we negotiate deadlines all the time. We let the editor know that in
order to do our best work for him, we'll need an extra few days so we're
not rushing through two assignments at once. That way we stress the benefits to *him* instead of the benefits to *us*. We can't recall a single instance
where the editor couldn't give us a little extra time.

Word Count

Sometimes an editor will assign you an idea you pitched—but she
wants it at 300 words, while you were envisioning a multi-page feature.
The editor does know her magazine and her audience better than you do,
but that doesn't mean you can't try talking her into a longer piece. You
probably won't change a short into a 3,000-word feature, but you may be
able to squeeze a couple hundred extra words out of the assignment.

Again, give reasons: "Do you have room for a longer piece on this? I'd
like to include two women who have experienced this problem plus expert tips on how readers can overcome it themselves. With a lede, two
stories, and three tips, I was thinking more along the lines of 600 words. I
totally understand if you still want a short, but I thought I'd ask." Do

make sure the word count you suggest fits into the magazine's format. In the example here, the magazine might have one-page department pieces that run around 600 words.

Payment Terms

Some magazines pay on publication, which means you don't get a check until the article is published. So if the magazine keeps pushing your article off to future issues, you don't get paid. If the magazine goes under before it runs your article, you also don't get paid.

If an editor offers you a pay-on-publication contract, you can either negotiate for pay on acceptance, or ask the editor to include in the contract the expected publication date and make sure it says that that's when you'll get paid no matter what. Some editors won't budge, though, and you'll need to decide whether it's worth it for you to do the assignment. Linda wrote for a long time for one pay-on-pub magazine, but she had enough pay-on-acceptance gigs in the pipeline that she didn't need to worry about the lag time. (See "BREAK THIS RULE: Never accept a pay-on-publication contract" later in this chapter.)

You Choose!

You can ask to add some clauses of your own, as well. After talking with her sister-in-law, an independent consultant, about how contracts work in other industries, Diana considered adding a clause to all future contracts that reads, "Payments made net 10 receive 1 percent discount." What that means is if the publisher issues you a check within 10 days of the invoice date, they can lop off one percent of the total invoice. Hey, Diana's willing to take a one percent pay cut for the privilege of fast cash. Such invoice discount schemes are common in the business world, and the magazine's printer probably offers such a discount for prompt payers, so why shouldn't writers follow suit?

The "rule" that you shouldn't negotiate contract details with your editors for fear they'll rescind the offer? Busted. You're a service provider, not a supplicant. Don't agree to write an article (or a blog post, or anything else) until you know and are fine with the terms of the assignment, from the pay to the deadline to the rights you're selling. You may have to walk away from some assignments, but that's okay. There will be more.

Turning down less-than-ideal assignments makes room for better ones to flow in.

BREAK THIS RULE

Assume you're getting the contract all writers get.

If an editor sends you a rights-grabbing contract, before signing on the dotted line, make sure they don't have a more writer-friendly one you can request. Magazines often have two contracts: the rapacious one they foist on new, inexperienced writers that asks them to sign away the rights to everything except the clothes they're wearing, and a more reasonable one for the experienced pros who know to ask. You want the reasonable one. It's best to do some homework before you get to the contract stage so you're not put on the spot with a terrible contract.

How to do this? Check around with your network, or if you belong to an online writing community like the Freelance Writers Den, ask whether any of the members have worked for the magazine before and what kind of contract they signed. Then you can ask for the contract your writer friends have been offered—or, if that seems too up-front for you, you can say, "Gee, the contract you gave me is an all-rights contract, and I want to sell only First North American Serial Rights," and see if they offer a different contract.

When Eric landed an assignment from a gaming magazine, he was dissatisfied with the all-rights terms. He asked whether the editor would buy first rights instead, and the editor quickly sent him a first-rights contract. The magazine obviously had two contracts on hand and sent writers the more restrictive one first as a matter of course.

It also helps to have a game plan in place if the editor insists the contract she's offered you is the only one they have—take it or leave it. Are you prepared to walk? Take it from us, it can be hard to say, "No thanks" and head for hills, especially when money's tight and bills are piling up. That's why it's essential to a) research how the magazine negotiates with writers and b) know what rights you're willing to sign away and what rights you aren't.

BREAK THIS RULE

Never sign an all-rights contract.

Many writers make a huge deal about retaining the rights to their articles, but sometimes it makes sense to take the money and run. Diana has signed all-rights contracts and will do so in the future if she decides the article has no resale value.

As an example, Diana wrote several columns for a technical publication about job opportunities for software programmers with specific skill sets at a particular point in time. Since the economy is always in flux and computer skill sets can go from hot to cold in a matter of months, she knew she wouldn't be able to sell the columns elsewhere. Instead, she traded all rights for a higher per-word pay rate.

Linda is pretty lazy about selling reprints these days; she doesn't enjoy revisiting a topic once she's done writing about it, and often writes articles for industry trades that would be difficult to resell—so she signs the contract, cashes the check, and moves on to the next assignment.

Even if a publisher buys all rights, you can still use your research to spin off article ideas for other magazines. Freelance writer Jennifer Weeks writes for an educational publisher in Washington, DC, that buys all rights to her work. "The contract is all-rights, but each issue is a month-long chunk of work for me and pays what I'm currently aiming to make in a month," she says. "Since it's a general reference magazine for students, researchers, and journalists, writing an issue gives me a stack of info on a subject in the news, which I can then draw on to spin off more specific articles. I've already gotten one assignment that's a spin-off of the issue I just wrote on oil and gas development, and have more proposals pending with editors."

You've negotiated a contract to your liking; now you can sit back and relax.

Au contraire. Publications can be quite sneaky about changing their contracts. Linda once called an editor because her check, which was due within 30 days of acceptance, was two weeks late. "You're mistaken," said the editor. "We pay on publication."

Confused, Linda checked her most recent contract and discovered that the magazine, which was experiencing cash flow problems, had stealthily changed the contract from pay-on-acceptance to pay-on-publication without telling Linda about the change.

The moral of the story: Read every contract, even if you've worked for the magazine dozens of times already, and question your editor about any changes that look unsavory.

BREAK THIS RULE

Don't ask an editor about money.

We writers would rather ask about word counts and due dates than ask the really important question: "How much do you pay and when can I expect my check?"

Sadly, a few editors do feel that a writer is being demanding and unreasonable if they want to know what they'll be paid before writing (or before pitching). On MediaBistro several years back, Colman Andrews, a sometimes-freelancer and the co-founder of *Saveur* magazine, wrote an article insisting that writers should never ask an editor what the magazine's pay range is before pitching. This is in part because, as he says, "I like to have the flexibility to reward particularly good writers (and, by extension, penalize those who simply meet the contract, if that)."

However, while it may be in editors' best interests to decide what to pay you *after* you've written a piece, it's certainly not in yours. As a businessperson with bills to pay, you need to talk dollars up front.

Nothing is more discouraging than going through the whole rigmarole of landing an assignment, even starting to write, and then discovering that the editor offers the non-negotiable rate of "exposure." The only way you can make an informed decision on whether to accept an assignment is to ask the editor about pay before she launches into her spiel about due dates, word counts, and topic slants. Rest assured she won't suddenly yank away the assignment because you asked what the pay rate would be...and if she's one of the rare ones who *would* do such a thing, you don't want to work with her anyway.

You can avoid the problem altogether by investigating the magazine's pay rates before you pitch the editor. Contact other writers in your network and ask them how they've fared payment-wise, keeping in mind that the direct question of, "How much did they pay you?" can be quite off-putting to most people. Get around this by asking questions like, "Did the magazine pay promptly?" "Was the editor willing to budge on a quoted rate?" These kinds of questions are more likely to elicit a solid figure better than asking, "How much did you get from that article in *OUT* magazine?" But even if they don't offer that information, you can probably figure out if the magazine is worth approaching by what they *do* tell you.

BREAK THIS RULE

Don't work without a contract.

Every writing expert will tell you that you must secure a contract if you want to be sure you'll be paid. But we Renegades beg to differ.

Let's face it: Contracts offered by publications mostly protect the magazine's rights, not yours. For example, many contracts give the magazine all rights to your article. But according to the NWU, if you have no contract, the magazine is automatically purchasing only First North American Serial Rights—meaning the rights revert back to you after publication and you can sell reprints of the article. And you know that awful clause in many contracts that says you're legally and financially responsible should a reader of said article sue the magazine for any reason? (That's the indemnification clause we talked about earlier.) If you don't have a contract, you don't have that clause.

However, we don't mean for you to work without any sort of assurance you'll get paid. *Do* get a written record of the assignment if the editor doesn't offer you a contract. Save the original assignment email—the one where the editor tells you what the article is about and how much and when you'll get paid. If your editor doesn't volunteer an assignment letter, ask for one or write one up yourself and ask him to approve it. If you run into a problem down the pike, you'll have something in writing to fall back on.

BREAK THIS RULE

Never accept a pay-on-publication contract.

Imagine this: You find a nice formal outfit at a local clothing store, but instead of whipping out your credit card, you tell the cashier you'll pay for the suit only should an occasion arise when you actually wear it.

Sounds silly, right? But that's the same situation writers face every day when they're offered assignments from markets that pay on publication instead of on acceptance. These pubs offer an assignment, accept the article, edit the piece, hold it until print time, publish it—and then, *finally*, pay the writer. And that's assuming the publication doesn't change its editorial focus or go under before the article makes it to print.

There's no way to know whether a market pays on publication or on acceptance until you look at its contract, unless this is mentioned in its *Writer's Digest* listing. Though you'd expect only smaller markets with little financing to pay on publication, this often isn't the case. "You can't generalize," says Dian Killian, former journalism division organizer for the National Writer's Union. Websites often pay on publication, but that's because many of them post articles so quickly that it's impossible for them to pay before publication.

Editors offer several reasons for paying on publication instead of on acceptance. Some markets, for example, are on tight budgets and need time to earn the money to pay writers. Pay-on-publication is also an easier system since the accounting department can pay all their writers at once instead of dealing with invoices spread throughout the payment period.

Finally, there's the CYA aspect: Editors don't want to put out money for something they may not be able to use. "In our case, as a custom publisher, we must let our clients approve manuscripts and design, and at any point they could decide to pull something or change something. That almost never happens, but it is an option for them which would leave us with having paid for something we then could not use," says Rebecca Rolfes, former editorial director for Imagination Publishing. "Kill fees are, of course, part of our contract, but we can't tie up our editorial dollars for articles that clients may want to drop or hold until later."

Editors may have their reasons for pay-on-pub, but that doesn't make it any easier for writers who accept such contracts. After all, as the name implies, if your article never makes it to publication—even through no fault of your own—you won't see one dollar, or at most will receive a kill fee. "I was burned by a new publication that insisted on paying only upon publication, but they assured me that they would run my article in a couple of months," says Maureen Dixon, a former freelance magazine writer. "The publication folded—of course—the month my article was slated to run."

Even if the magazine doesn't go belly-up, publication lead times are often six months or more, and that's a long time to wait to be paid. What's more, even if you sell First North American Serial rights to an article, you can't sell reprints of it until it's actually been published, which curtails your money-making power even more. That's why both the NWU and ASJA urge writers to reject pay-on-pub contracts.

On the other hand, if you have enough pay-on-acceptance assignments that you can afford to wait for a check from one magazine, you can profit. Linda, for example, wrote regularly for one magazine that pays on publication, and she never had a problem getting paid. Payment would sometimes take a *long* time, but it would always come.

If you do decide to write for magazines that pay on publication, take these steps to protect yourself:

Negotiate.

Perhaps the magazine will be willing to bend the contract for you.

Get a firm date.

If the editor won't change the pay-on-pub terms, you may be able to get her to include the expected date of publication in the contract so that you have some idea of what your cash flow will look like in the future. Or better yet, ask whether you can be paid after X number of days or on publication, whichever comes first.

Demand your fee.

Make sure that if the publication changes direction before your article is published and decides not to run your piece through no fault of your own, you'll still be paid. Because it can take so long between acceptance and publication/payment, chances of this happening are higher than with pay-on-acceptance contracts.

Lessen your risk.

You stand less of a chance of getting burned (and any burns will hurt less) if you stick with the familiar and the small, according to freelance writer Kelly James. "I write pay-on-pub for two types of magazines," she says. "Smaller magazines where I have an ongoing relationship with the editors and write for them every issue, and magazines that purchase reprints to stories." Diana will accept a pay-on-pub contract only if the dollar amount is under $500, so if for some reason her article is never published, at least she's not out thousands.

Diversify.

Writing for a few pay-on-pub magazines won't make your financial situation sticky if you can rely on a steady influx of checks from publications that pay on acceptance.

Pay-on-pub contracts may not be a boon for writers, but neither are they a bane that will automatically crush your career. Play it smart, negotiate, and don't plan your budget around pay-on-pub assignments—and you can profit from writing for these magazines.

BREAK THIS RULE

Never agree to write on spec.

The usual practice is to pitch an editor and *then* write the article once you get an assignment. The upside to this is that the editor can tell you exactly what she wants. The downside to this, for new writers, is that if you have no clips to show the editor, she has no way of telling if you can pull off an assignment. So she'd be taking a *huge* risk in offering a contract without proof you can do the work.

Many writers spread the "rule" that you should never, ever write on spec. On spec is short for "on speculation," and it means you write the article without a contract or any promise of payment, and then the editor decides if she'd like to buy it. This removes the risk from the editor and places it directly onto the writer.

It's often a bad idea to accept an on-spec assignment since you'll be writing an article that's slanted for a particular publication without any promise of eventual payment; because you wrote it to the editor's specifications, it's unlikely you'll be able to sell it elsewhere should it be rejected. You have to ask yourself if you're willing and able to take on a risk like that.

But sometimes you *have* to take risks to jumpstart your writing career, and writing on spec—maybe once or twice—if an editor asks can be a good way to get your foot in the door of a magazine if you don't have any clips. (Also, don't forget the concept of the "on spec query" we talked about in Chapter 3.)

Never accept less than $1 per word.

What is it with the magic $1 per word rate all writers seem to strive for? We've had $1 per word (and more!) assignments where we'd have been better off grinding beans at Starbucks for an afternoon.

For example, Linda used to write for a print magazine that paid a whopping $1.75 per word, but the rate tells only half the story. Once she spent a ton of time researching and writing a health article for this magazine. Two weeks later the editor emailed to ask Linda to provide prices for all the medical procedures mentioned in the article. So Linda called specialists around the country, many of whom were reluctant to reveal their fees. A week later, the editor emailed again: She wanted Linda to combine two sections. A week after that, the editor sent back the article riddled with more questions that needed to be answered.

The bottom line: With the hourly rate Linda earned on this article, she would have been better off writing for a trade magazine. In fact, at the same time, Linda had a regular gig writing project profiles for a technology trade. The pay was only about 25 cents per word, but because it took her only an hour and a half to do the interview and write each piece, Linda actually earned $160 per hour.

Diana also took this "dollars per hour" approach to heart when she wrote "shorts," 200- to 500-word articles, for *Psychology Today* for the so-so sum of 50 cents per word. Her editor would provide story ideas based on recent psychological studies and even provide the source's contact information, so all Diana had to do was call the source and summarize the research. It never took more than two hours total to do the work, which meant she was making $100 to $200 per hour. Not bad!

The moral of the story is, *don't* write off lower-paying assignments merely because they're not in the magic $1-per-word league; these assignments can boost your cash flow quite nicely if you write them quickly and get paid equally fast, and sometimes they can even lead to much bigger financial paydirt in the long run. "Against the advice of peers and family, I occasionally write for a local alt news editor who pays about 12 cents per word for complex 5,000 word cover stories," says freelancer Wendy Lyons Sunshine. "She's a great editor and gave me a terrific break early on, but continuing to write for her is akin to charity financially—or so I thought."

Once the editor came to Wendy with a hot lead about local experts doing exciting research, and she couldn't resist accepting the assignment. "By the time the article appeared, these experts—whose renown is skyrocketing within their field—had invited me to collaborate with them on their first mainstream book," she says. "I've just finished the book proposal and quickly had interest from agents. Not only are the experts simply wonderful to work with, but because I had already reported on their work in depth, drafting the proposal went easily, and the payment for that was many times what I earned on the original article! Maybe the odds of this happening are akin to a lightning strike, but low-priced work led me to opportunities, and income, I never expected!"

The problem arises when you accept 25-cent-per-word assignments that take several solid days to research and write—and worse, you get an editor who makes you rewrite it a few times. Eventually you'll start to develop a sense for pain-in-the-butt editors and publications, and can either negotiate for more money or walk away.

BREAK THIS RULE

Don't ask for better contract terms or the editor may take your assignment away.

This isn't a rule—this is your fear speaking. Very, very rarely will an editor rescind an offer because you asked for changes to the contract terms.

Besides, would you really want to work for someone who gets hot under the collar whenever a professional service provider negotiates a contract? Most editors expect negotiation and may even be surprised if you roll over and play dead with the first terms they give you. Editors understand what freelancers are up against since many of them freelance on the side, and often they'll work with you—even if it's only to tell you they're sorry that they can't change the terms, but they'll make sure you're paid quickly. Maybe they'll throw extra money in the pot to sweeten the deal, but you'll never know until you ask.

When an editor offers an assignment, don't haggle over the pay rate.

At a writers' convention, Linda was shocked to hear a freelancer say she's worked in the industry for 25 years and has never asked an editor for more money. The mind boggles! This is another "rule" spurred by fear, not logic.

While you're negotiating with an editor over rights, deadlines, and other details, don't be afraid to mention money. Years ago Linda sent the following email to her editor at *Family Circle*: "I've written several articles for you, and you seem happy with my work. Do you think you could swing a pay raise for my next assignment?" The editor got back to her in a day and offered her a 50 percent pay hike! She also told Linda to not tell other writers, as Linda was now the highest-paid writer at the magazine.

Stoked by her success, Linda used the same tactic with her editor at *Oxygen*. The editor didn't match FC's raise, but she did offer a 10-cent-per-word raise. This might not sound like much, but for every 1,000 words, Linda now earned an extra $100 just because she asked for it.

Does the idea of negotiating make you want to dive under the covers? Try these tips to up your negotiating power:

Don't say "yes" right away.

If an editor calls to offer a contract, you can get all the details, but you don't have to commit at that moment. Tell the editor you'll get back to her in a few hours or the next day, hang up, give your kid a high-five, and then do some quick research with your network to be sure you're being offered a fair rate and that the editor is someone you'd want to work with.

"That seems a little low to me..."

The National Writers Union credits journalist Brett Harvey with coining this phrase, and we've met many other journalists who use it (or a variation thereof) after an editor offers an unsavory rate. It helps if you practice saying the phrase so that you sound strong and confident, not weak and unsure.

The other key to using this phrase is to keep your mouth shut after you've put it out there. Even if you experience a few moments of uncomfortable silence, let your editor be the first to respond. There's no need to plead, "My cat has this hairball problem and I need to start buying her an expensive brand of food, so please, please, please pay me more." You can also use this phrase in email negotiations—it's even better, in fact, because you don't have to worry about pregnant pauses.

Practice.

Once you've gone through a few of these assignment phone calls (and we hope you get lots of them!) you'll discover they generally follow the same script. Your editor will talk about the assignment itself—what he expects, what he'd like to see in your finished piece, etc.—and then move to those more mundane matters, like due dates. Diana has found in some cases she has to *ask* about payment! The editors always sound a bit flustered after Diana asks, "And how much are you offering for this piece?"

If you get all muddled about asking for more money or better contract terms, practice with your partner, with a friend in your network, or even in front of a mirror. Or put yourself in the shoes of a master negotiator who always comes out on top. Imagine how she would respond to a low-ball offer and adapt that attitude in your own real-life dealings.

"No one has ever complained about our contract."

We cringe when an editor spews this "rule" out. Not because we're ashamed of ourselves for having the audacity to ask for an extra 25 bucks for electronic rights, but because it's akin to the editor claiming like a 6-year-old, "Everyone else is doing it this way, so why can't you?"

If an editor throws this at you during the negotiation phase, you can assure yourself of three things:

1. It's a bully move. Trust us, you're *not* the first writer to stand up to him.
2. In the highly unlikely event you *are* the first writer to ask him for contract changes, it's because he graduated from college last month and this is his first editorial job.
3. He's putting you on the defensive and assuming you'll fold because, you know, writers = wimps. Instead of feeling ashamed (about yourself, for asking), you should feel annoyed (with him, for being a jerk).

There are a couple of ways to handle this comment and others like it. You can ignore it, pretending it's not out there. Or you can reply, "Hmm, that's interesting." Pause. "Now back to what we were discussing, how does an extra $100 sound?" And if you're feeling so-so about the assignment, you could respond with something cheeky like, "Really? I've never had a problem making this change in other contracts."

Don't let comments like these derail you from your goal. If an editor continues to lob verbal grenades at you during negotiations, it could be his way of intimidating you into accepting the status quo, and maybe you need to rethink how much you really want to work with someone who operates like this. After all, if he's this bullying about a few changes to some legalese, what's he going to be like when he's editing your copy? If you're getting a bad feeling in the pit of your stomach about the editor's interpersonal skills, maybe it's best to take your talents elsewhere. Don't be afraid to walk away.

RENEGADE RULE-BREAKER

Jenna Schnuer

Jenna Schnuer has been a full-time freelance magazine writer for nearly 20 years and has written for publications many writers have on their bucket lists: *National Geographic Traveler*, *Rolling Stone*, *Smithsonian*, and more (www.jennaschnuer.com). For the past three years, she has been living and building her career in Anchorage, Alaska, 4,431 miles away from her (always) hometown of NYC and the hubbub of the New York media world.

What led you to go freelance?

I never seriously considered becoming a freelance writer. I always thought I'd be a staff person. In 1999, I had an incredibly interesting job as an editor at iVillage's Book Channel in New York City. It was an exciting time—the company had just gone public, the internet was exploding, there was money in publishing—and one day a friend called me and said, "Hey, I have a six-week project for you, but you'll have to quit your job and go freelance if you want it." The project sounded interesting and engaging, so I gave my two weeks at iVillage. A big part of who I am is a person who takes chances, who wants to pursue interesting opportunities. I bought a desk and a laptop, shoved them against the only open wall in my Upper East Side studio, and went to work. That was 18 years ago, and it was the best unexpected decision I've ever made.

Tell us about a writing rule you break and how breaking it benefits your career.

I call myself "an unapologetic generalist." Even though I write a lot of travel stories, I don't think of myself as a "travel writer" but as a writer who finds stories when she travels. A lot of advice you hear is that you should specialize or become known as a travel writer or science writer or health and fitness writer if you want to make any money freelancing, but I'm the kind of writer who wants to make a living writing stories that interest me. It's key for me staying in this job as long as I have, because if I were specializing to make more money, freelancing wouldn't be as interesting to me anymore. Plus, I think it's too difficult a job to be in it just to make lots of money though, of course, making money is a lovely thing to do. There are easier ways out there to get rich!

What are your biggest challenges as a freelancer?

For me, writing is a confidence game. I have to really work to keep my confidence up. Some of the things I do when I'm not feeling bright and shiny is reading some of my old query letters that have sold. It reminds me that I do have something to say that magazines want to hear...and buy! I also volunteer and teach; sharing my knowledge with those who are just starting out shows me the value of the experience I've gained during my career. I also like to talk to people. Nothing gets me more excited than talking to an interesting source or meeting someone who gets me back to the place of "This is why I write."

Another challenge I faced was more recent; I was diagnosed with cancer 11 months after moving to Alaska. I'm single and self-employed, so I had to work throughout my treatment. I could not *not* work. I was honest with my editors about my health, and because the publishing world is filled with some really wonderful, kind human beings (yes, really!), they were understanding about my treatment and energy levels. They called me with assignments, and they were good about giving me work that didn't require an enormous amount of research or reporting. In many ways, freelancing was the ideal job to have while going through my cancer treatment because I could work when I had the energy and rest when I needed it. [Editorial note: Jenna is two years out of treatment and doing well. Take *that*, stupid cancer!]

The real challenge has been that cancer stopped my momentum. For example, I was deep in talks with *Smithsonian* about a feature assignment right around the time I was diagnosed, but then when I couldn't travel, they had to cut it down to a FOB (front-of-book) piece, which was disappointing. It has taken some time for the fog of "chemo brain" (it's real!) to wear off, and I'm getting back to a place where I feel like I'm "me" again.

What do you know now that you wish you knew when you were starting out?

When I started out, like a lot of freelancers I worked every single day, including weekends and nights. Looking back, I don't think that was good for me. Maybe it's because I'm older, but I've come to see that I want my life to wrap around my job and not my job to wrap around my life.

There's nothing more discouraging than when I see a writer on Facebook announcing they're so busy they have to work late nights and weekends. I'm like, "Ugh. Humble brag cloaked as *poor me*." If you're sitting in front of a computer all the time, you're not out there living. I think it's important to work, but also to take time to do stuff you enjoy or that makes you healthier. Take up a hobby. Go to the movies...see a movie that has nothing to do with your life. Enjoy walks with your dog. Talk to people.

What advice can you offer a mid-career writer who feels stuck, burned out, or discouraged?

When I'm feeling "off" in my job, I ask my favorite editors and close friends "Hey, tell me what I'm good at. What about my work resonates with you?" So much of this job is about making yourself stand out from other writers, so hearing affirmation from people who really know your work can give you a boost. You don't get a lot of career guidance as a freelancer: You don't have bosses or mentors pushing you, setting goals for your career, or watching over you. You've got to manage your own growth. Freelancing is a job where you can stay at the same level and do fine, but if you want to become better, you have to push yourself to find the editors or colleagues who'll tell you where you need to improve, who'll tell you the things you need to know to keep growing.

Then redo your collateral materials. Order some new business cards. Scroll through your website and read what you have there. Is there anything you can update? Take time to read some of your work; it's proof you *can* write, you *can* get assignments.

It's also important get inspired by other art and new ideas. Dive into something you've never tried or get back into a hobby or interest you had as a little kid. Right now I'm taking an online class to learn how to podcast. I think that could be an interesting outlet for me to tell my stories in a different way. Keep learning new stuff. When you're learning, it shakes up your brain and gets you thinking in a new direction.

CHAPTER 5

Mining for Information: A Little Digging Can Turn Up Info Gold

If you scramble to find sources for your articles, if you have trouble dealing with PR people, or if you moan over how costly database access is, this chapter is for you. Let's bust the rules that are keeping you from finding, and interviewing, the right sources for your pitches and articles.

BREAK THIS RULE

You must find original sources for every article.

Original sources are great, but hardly necessary. To find sources, look at other articles similar in subject to yours and take note of who is quoted. Journalist Alison Stein, former editor-at-large at *American Demographics*, notes who's quoted in *The New York Times* Week in Review section and adds relevant experts to her list of potential sources. These sources likely command respect in their fields, and she already knows they're willing to speak with the media.

Linda has done the same; when faced with an article assignment on, say, restaurant management, she searches online for similar articles and taps some of the experts there. The caveat is that you need to make sure the source isn't overexposed in the media—no one wants to interview the same source everyone else is using—and that they aren't the sole property of a competing publication.

You can even use your own published articles to find "new" sources! When Diana was pitching a story on pet etiquette to a women's magazine, she got quotes from an etiquette consultant she'd profiled for a career website. Then, when one of Diana's colleagues was looking for a young, hip etiquette expert to interview for an article in *Condé Nast Brides*, Diana had the perfect source for her.

BREAK THIS RULE

Find your own sources; don't ask your editor to help you.

A lot of writers miss a primo timesaving opportunity when they're talking over article assignments with their editors. They'll ask everything from how long the finished piece should be and when it will run, to how the editor would like it delivered. But they don't bother to ask, "Is there anyone you know who'd make a great source for this story?"

If you're writing an article for a trade magazine, or on a topic that's near and dear to the general readership of the publication, your editor will often have a contact list crammed with the names of experts, industry analysts he's met at trade shows, or authors who've written seminal books on the subject. Since editors have their fingers on the pulse of their readership, wouldn't it make sense to ask them for source suggestions?

Often, your editor will happily provide you with several names and appropriate contact information. Presto! Now you don't have to scramble around and spend hours digging for the names yourself. If your editor has spent time thinking about the right people with whom you should speak, often you'll be set for the whole article. This is why writing "shorts" can be so profitable for writers, especially if your editor is calling you with the assignments: Most of the time, you need only one source, and your editor will have this person picked out for you. All you have to do is call or email your handpicked source.

Sometimes your editor will give you sources that don't pan out. You can always go back to him and ask for more names, or ask the sources you've spoken with if they know anyone else who'd be willing to talk to you.

Rethink this strategy, however, when you're doing a piece where it's assumed you're the one who has the edge on appropriate sources. For example, if you're touting yourself as a health and fitness writer to a women's magazine, your editor would raise an eyebrow if you asked her for names of appropriate medical experts to interview. Another example would be if you've sold a proposal for a celebrity profile or a story featuring "people on the street." The editor will naturally assume that you already have access to the celebrity you're pitching, and it's your job to find the "real people" to interview.

BREAK THIS RULE

"Real people" don't want to be interviewed, so don't bother.

Take a look through a few consumer magazines. Within a few minutes you'll meet Tyler, 26, a New York City bartender who loves a good one-night stand, or Karen Smith, mom to Zachary, who wonders if her son is playing too much Pokémon Go.

When Diana teaches her course on freelance writing, her students worry about finding "real people" to quote in their articles. How do you find a bartender who serves up more than drinks? If students want to write for parenting magazines, they wonder how they'll find parents who'll talk to them. Do the writers actually already know these people?

If it's any consolation, many working writers kvetch about the insatiable appetites their editors have for anecdotes from "real people" sources. Sometimes it's a real pill finding the right person for an article, especially if your editor has asked you to quote "an attractive, fit woman between the ages of 30-35 who's willing to be photographed in a bikini from all angles—and living in 'flyover country.'" Yes, magazine writers often get tasked with these seemingly impossible requests!

It helps if you have a writing specialty. For example, Diana has written for magazines targeted to mothers of young children or women in their 30s and 40s. This meant her stories were peppered with anecdotes from mothers of young children or women in their 30s and 40s, so it behooved her to cultivate sources who fit these demographics. Business features will require quotes and stories from workers on the front lines or executives in their corner offices, depending on the focus of the magazine. Health stories may require tales of woe from patients suffering from a particular condition. If you want to write for a smart-alecky men's magazine, you'll want to quote smart-alecky men.

If you've had the opportunity to get near a newsroom, you'll see that beat reporters have contact lists filled with the names of people they can call for a quick quote. Want to wow your editors with your reporting skills? You, too, should work to fill your contact lists with the names of anxious young mothers, frustrated advertising executives, or snarky twenty-something males. And it helps if you can do this before you actually need to call on them. Here's how to gather up the "people on the street" sources who can add to sparkle to your pitches and articles:

Reach out to your friends, family, and neighbors online and ask them if they're willing to be sources in future articles.

Since this book was written in 2003 and updated in 2006, there's been an explosion in social media that makes it even easier to reach out to potential sources: Think Facebook, Twitter, Instagram, or blogs, to name a few of the obvious platforms. Some editors are fine with anecdotes and quotes from a writer's sister-in-law or best friend, but to keep things on the up-and-up, let your editor know the relationship ahead of time so she can make the conflict of interest call.

Develop an email list of friends and family you can tap for quotes.

If you send out a group email, be discreet and BCC (blind carbon copy) the email addresses. Your sources are entitled to privacy. Imagine how embarrassing it could be if your email starts, "You once mentioned to me that you think about cheating on your spouse. Are you willing to talk?" You're going to have a lot of angry people wanting to do more than talk.

Ask your Facebook friends to pass your request on to *their* friends.

For example, Diana's Florida-based sister-in-law put her request out to all the mothers who worked in the department of her university, and Diana ended up using a few of them as real-mom sources in her parenting articles. This helps eliminate the conflict of interest issue, since you're now reaching people you don't know.

Go out into the real world.

If you're writing business features, attend local networking events and industry conferences where you're apt to run into people who would make good sources. If you want to write about child development, bring your notebook with you next time you head off to the playground with your children. You'll be sure to bump into parents who'll be flattered when you ask, "Wow, I can't believe your 3-year-old speaks three languages! I'm a freelance writer—mind if I get your contact information so I can get a quote for a story on multilingual children?"

Check out internet newsgroups and forums related to the topics you're writing about.

These gathering places can be hostile to journalists, but neither Linda nor Diana has had their hands virtually slapped in cyberspace when they visited such places for the express purpose of finding sources. If you're a frequent, visible visitor to a website or bulletin board, you usually won't have any problem if you post a request for sources. If you don't visit often (or at all), contact the board's administrator and explain your request. Often that little courtesy will net you a warm welcome—and the admin might post the request himself, thus giving you greater legitimacy among readers.

Delve into your database of experts.

Expert sources, too, have families and health problems and quirky stories. Moreover, since they're used to speaking with the media, they're often more understanding of the publishing process—and they'll often go out of their way to help you find an elusive anecdote. One public relations representative Diana has worked with has also been quoted as a father in a *Parenting* story and as a former dieter in her weight-loss book. If you need to speak with a woman who is living with diabetes, then call your contact at the American Diabetes Association—chances are they'll know someone who fits your requirements or they'll be able to point you in the right direction.

Cast your net far and wide.

Unless you're writing for regional magazines, you'll want to find people all over the country—perhaps even abroad—for your stories. National magazine editors want to see quotes from people who live in places other than metropolitan New York City or other major coastal cities. And if you turn in a story quoting people who all live within a 50-mile radius of your apartment, your editor's going to question your reporting skills. When Diana and Linda write for national magazines, they may use one source who lives in Florida, another who's in Missouri, a third in Washington state, and the fourth from the northeast—but never all from California or New England. Likewise, if you're writing for a regional magazine that focuses on Midwest living, don't quote someone who lives in sunny Florida.

When you finally land your assignment, you'll have a ready stable of "real people" sources to call upon.

BREAK THIS RULE

Database access is too expensive for freelance writers.

The good news since we first wrote this book is that access to research and magazine databases is no longer available only to the select few who work in newsrooms or who have the funds to pay for it. Most anyone who lives in North America can tap into their local public library's magazine databases from home for free access to thousands of consumer and trade magazines. All it will cost you is one visit to your librarian for a library card, and maybe a stop at the reference desk for instructions. Diana's public library, for example, offers free access to the Gale Group's consumer magazine databases, as well as Zinio, which lets patrons read current and back issues of a number of consumer magazines.

Most major newspapers around the world have web-based searchable archives that go back years. If an article has been published recently, sometimes you can read it for free, but if it's older, you may have to pay a small fee for full-text access.

If you have a strong relationship with one of the publications you write for and they happen to have editorial offices nearby, you can ask whether they'll let you tap into their databases. Many publications have subscriptions to LexisNexis databases, so take advantage of your connections if you have them. Another option is to try a local college or university library, especially if you have an affiliation with them as a student, alum, teacher, or spouse of an employee.

BREAK THIS RULE

Your sources must be well-known experts in their fields.

Open up any magazine, and sure, you'll find multitudes of quotes from industry titans, media pundits, celebrities du jour, and doctors touting eponymous diet books. But look beyond the household names and you'll find as many expert quotes from people whose names are totally unfamiliar to you.

Your expert sources don't have to be newsprint regulars; in fact, no-name-brand quotes are often better. If you depend on ProfNet to find sources, it can be embarrassing when your editor informs you that the expert you've quoted in your article pops up in nearly every other article that crosses her desk. (The proactive solution? Do a quick search on your source to find out whether she's been quoted in the publication in the past.)

Believe it or not, no-name experts often give *better* quotes because they're not as used to talking to the media. We've spoken with self-proclaimed experts who've spent too much time hanging out with their PR handlers, and their quotes sound like they're on their umpteenth regurgitation. (This proves true most often when speaking with high-level business executives.) It is extremely difficult to get these people to give you a quote that's juicy and fresh and that doesn't sound like it was written by their corporate communications department and vetted by their attorneys.

The key to locating great sources is to not only exploit services like ProfNet, but to mine your everyday life. When Diana landed an assignment from *Walking* about massage anxiety, she did the expected, which was to call the press contact for the American Massage Therapy Association. They put her in contact with several therapists around the country, all of whom were practiced interviewees. But then Diana also interviewed her own massage therapist, a woman who'd never been interviewed before. Diana's masseuse ended up giving her the key quote for her article.

If you're working on a story that features real people and not experts, turn to your personal database of sources—which we described how to build in a previous section—and send a BCC'd email out to all. You can also ask everyone you bump into if they know of people who can help you out: Your hairdresser, doctor, or therapist, for example, can be goldmines of information.

When Diana was pitching parenting articles, she pestered everyone in her mothers' group and her son's playgroups for potential sources—not to mention story ideas! She also talked to her son's pediatrician about the best medical experts for certain stories. While working on a pitch about children and chronic back pain, Diana noticed a letter to the editor in her local paper from a parent who was concerned about the weight of his son's backpack. A quick search gave Diana the letter writer's telephone number, so she called him and got great "man on the street" quotes from him for her proposal.

BREAK THIS RULE

People are who they say they are. No need to double-check!

The freelancers we know are generally amiable, curious writers who passionately believe in truth and honesty, but not every person they interview believes as passionately in truth and honesty as they do.

When you find an expert source, do a little detective work before you interview him. For example, say you're looking for an expert on vegetarian nutrition through ProfNet and one of the experts who responds to your query says he's a professor and the author of four books. Sounds great! But before you schedule that interview, check him out. You may find he's an adjunct professor of humanities and his four books are about George Bernard Shaw. Okay, so George Bernard Shaw was a vegetarian, but that doesn't make your professor a nutritional expert on vegetarianism.

Some "experts" will do anything to get publicity, including fudging their credentials or withholding information that might indicate a conflict of interest. When Diana was writing her diet book, she found a research scientist who had interesting things to say about a certain wonder food. However, a five-minute Google search revealed that this scientist was on a board that promoted said wonder food; what's more, he was being slammed by consumer groups for his corporate ties. She gave this guy the boot and interviewed a more impartial nutritional expert. Once you have a little experience, you'll soon learn how to spot compromised experts and move on to sources who truly can provide the expertise you need.

Another caution: Many magazines do not like to quote the same expert sources over and over again. One of the magazines Diana writes for has a little-known rule that an expert can be quoted only once within the same year. Other magazines don't want experts who are regularly quoted in competing magazines. You can ask your source, "Have you been quoted in *Goat Farming Monthly* in the last year?" but don't count on getting an honest answer. We've had experts assure us that they've never been quoted in Magazine X, only to discover through an archives search that they were featured prominently six months earlier. Or we'll tell our editor, "I was thinking about interviewing Dr. X for this article on enuresis" and she'll laugh and say, "Not him again! I have three articles on my desk he's quoted in." Some experts will tell you what you want to hear if it gets their name in print, so keep your BS detector finely tuned when you're sourcing.

BREAK THIS RULE

Rely on public relations reps;
they're there to help you write the best article.

PR agencies and departments answer to their clients, not to you. Sure, they'll act like they're your new BFFs, especially if you're writing a cover story for a big newsstand magazine that bathes their client or their client's products in a flattering light. But woe to those writers who depend solely on the kindness of PR departments or agencies when writing for a smaller magazine or about a touchy subject that won't benefit their client.

Here's a cautionary tale: Diana took on a cover story about how staffing agencies account for the high hourly markups on consultant time even though she knew it was going to be difficult to get staffing firms to talk. First of all, the magazine's audience was made up of IT consultants, the people who were purportedly being screwed by these agencies. Second, the agencies would have to explain in detail how they came up with their markup numbers, and they'd have to share this proprietary information not only with consultants, but also with competitors reading the magazine. The agencies gained nothing by speaking with Diana about this subject.

She tracked down sources and plotted a strategy to get staffing firms to talk. Her editor said that as a last resort, Diana could agree with her sources that quotes would not be attributed to them and that their firms would not be identified by name in the story. She also made sure that the PR people knew up front what she was looking for so that there would be no surprises during the interviews.

One associate for a PR firm representing a staffing agency was all over Diana like a fly on honey. Of course the president of the company was willing to talk! Everything was moving along smoothly until a few minutes before the scheduled interview. That's when the PR rep called and nervously asked if Diana could forward her the questions for review.

With foreboding in her heart, she sent an overview of what she was looking for, the same overview she'd sent the rep a week before. A few minutes later, the PR rep sent an email saying that the company president was sorry, but he had to leave his office suddenly. Poof! Both were never to be heard from again.

This scenario or variations thereof can happen, and usually when you've got a tight deadline, so beware. Many PR professionals, especially those fresh out of college, set up interviews with reporters as if they've got a quota for the month. They'll volunteer their clients for *anything* ("My client, the leading provider of email filtering software, is the perfect source for your article on new developments in dandruff control!"), but when the client is apprised of the topic, he backs out of the interview—and rightfully so. We've done far too many interviews where the interviewee is at a complete loss as to why he's talking to us. It's a total waste of his time, as well as ours, and we're not happy with the PR rep afterwards.

Once you start working on lots of assignments, you'll need to manage your PR contacts. We suggest that you set up several free email accounts. This will allow you to give PR contacts an alternative email address so you won't have to sift through tons of boring press releases to read your regular email. Diana has the ability to create as many email addresses as she wants with her web domain name. When she posts a query at ProfNet, for example, she creates a new address that's relevant to the story she's currently working on—a story on kids and pet allergies, for example, might have an address such as allerpetpress@ninetofive.com.

Occasionally, a PR firm will start bombarding her with press releases months later; by checking the email address they've used, Diana can tell whether they're using her address improperly and blacklist them. You can also look into getting a throwaway email address that works for a limited amount of time before it self-destructs or until you're done with your story. Hit delete, and the email address vanishes so you won't notice if you've been added to PR mailing lists.

BREAK THIS RULE

PR people are your enemies.

Based on our last rule breaker, you're probably thinking we don't have a whit of respect for the PR profession. Wrong! Yes, a few flakes and kooks exist, but let's be fair: PR reps can match our horror stories with tales of freelance writers who have flaked out on *them*. The bottom line is that at some point in your freelancing career, you'll have to go through a PR agency or rep to get to your source, and you need to learn how to work with these generally affable folks. Don't forget that you need them as much as they need you.

Diana has a unique perspective on the writer/agency/source relationship, because she used to be the person journalists scrambled to reach when they needed a quote for breaking news in the household adhesives market. Whenever the media called her company, they were forwarded to an account executive at her company's retained public relations firm for screening.

PR agencies are looking to get their clients the best possible coverage, so if a writer representing a big-name publication like *Better Homes & Gardens* or *This Old House* approached the agency, they would be whisked to the interview table. Reporters from key trade publications also got this kind of snap-to-it service. But after that, there was a definite pecking order as to which journalists got through and which ones didn't. A feature writer from a small newspaper chain in northern Minnesota would not get this kind of attention, and a freelancer who didn't have a firm assignment from a publication would get even less. Usually, the PR agency would send a press kit to these folks, or give them quotes as the company's official representatives.

So, if you've got a firm assignment from a major publication, you'll probably have no trouble getting PR reps to take your calls and set up appointments with their clients. But what if you fall in that second or third tier of writers? If you really need to get through to a key source, and you feel that the PR agency is running interference, how can you get them to listen to you?

The key is to position your request so that it's in the PR agency's best interests to help you. Don't expect them to puzzle out what those interests are, or you'll soon find yourself holding one of their client's press kits filled with boring, corporate-speak copy.

Let's make up an example: You're pitching a story to a parenting magazine about whether or not babies benefit from "educational apps" marketed to their overachieving parents. You'd love to quote the founder of a top educational toy company, but overprotective flacks guard her. In your request to her company's PR department, be honest—tell them you're developing an idea or writing a pitch. We know a few writers who've lied and said they had an assignment only to have it backfire when the suspicious PR rep called the magazine to confirm. How embarrassing!

If parenting and education are your beats, make sure they know that, and tell them what other magazines you've worked with. If you don't do this, you're losing a great opportunity to convince them that it's in their future best interests to set up this interview for you, even if this interview doesn't guarantee press for their client. If you don't have this kind of ammo, then put the best possible spin on your request. How many people will be reading your article? If the founder doesn't speak with you, will it reflect poorly on her company? Are her competitors giving you quotes?

Once you have their attention, make sure they know what you need from their client. Often, PR reps will ask you for the questions ahead of time: They'll say their client needs them to prepare. Ninety-nine percent of the time, we'll oblige (see "BREAK THIS RULE: Don't send your questions to the source"). If you think that not providing the questions will be a deal-breaker and you really need this interview, go ahead and do so, keeping in mind you're certainly free to ask any question you like during the actual interview. At any rate, we like to provide PR reps with an overview of what we're looking for ahead of time so they can prepare their client for an efficient and informative interview.

When you're dealing with a PR agency, it's a good bet they've done a lot of work to set up the interview for you, especially if the person you're speaking with is a high-level executive. Make sure you call when you're supposed to, not five minutes later. Often, the agency will ask if they can call you because they want to patch the source in with the PR agency listening in on the interview. Some agencies will insist on listening in, usually so they can later coach their client on how to answer any questions he flubbed. If you want to fight that, that's your call. Diana doesn't mind the eavesdropping—often, the rep will point something important out that the client has forgotten to mention.

It's not difficult to develop a negative attitude toward public relations professionals, because when they screw a writer over, they usually screw them over big time. So when we meet a PR person who has done a great job setting up interviews, providing helpful information, and prepping his client for a productive interview, we go out of our way to thank him and make him feel appreciated.

BREAK THIS RULE

You have to go through the PR agency/department.

Many journalists automatically search for the telephone number of the PR department to make initial contact with a source. Reconsider this. The PR department, not your source, will then decide whether or not your interview is worthy of the source's time. At best, the PR department can take a few days to get back to you...bad news if you're under a tight deadline. At worst, your request gets buried under all the other requests they're fielding, especially if the company or organization attracts a lot of publicity.

If you have the name of the person you want to talk to, skip the PR people and call or email her directly with your request. Sometimes she'll give you the information you need right on the phone. Other times she'll tell you she can't talk until she clears it with her superiors. Even then, that's better than relying on a third-party to set up initial contact.

Diana once interviewed some extremely busy magazine editors for an article. She did a little research, found a few editors who could speak knowledgeably on the topic, then contacted them directly. One editor asked for the questions and answered them by email. The second editor needed to clear things with her boss first, but approval to speak came within a day. The third answered Diana's questions, and actually gave the questions to her boss to answer, too!

Had Diana gone through the appropriate PR channels, she believes she'd still be waiting for the seas to part, the heavens to open, and the angels to belt out "Hallelujah." The worst that can happen is that your source will ask you go through her PR department or agency, but even then, you'll have more leverage when you approach these PR people with a warmed-up source on your side.

You can never have too many sources or too much research for a story.

Ah, the classic rationalization of an inveterate procrastinator. Reading back issues, surfing the web, emailing potential sources—all these things feel productive, and they are...to a certain point.

We succumb to this time-sucking rule when we're writing for a new editor or publication, and we want to impress them with our reporting skills. We'll search a database for one more study, one more factoid that will make our article sound more authoritative. Or maybe one or two more expert quotes will provide more balance. We fall into this trap when we're tackling a subject we've never covered before or a lengthy assignment where we have more leeway on content.

With long, fact-intensive pieces, Diana stops doing research when she notices that her sources start sounding alike, and the new quotes and information she's getting parrots what she's already researched. She also keeps the length of her article in mind when she's looking for sources—a 200-word short requires only one source, while a 2,000-word technology story may require five or six sources. One good rule of thumb is to interview one person for every 500 words, plus one more for good measure. So a 500-word article will have two sources, and a 1,500-word piece will have four.

Another tip for chronic over-researching is to write down the list of questions your article absolutely must answer, and look at those questions frequently when you're researching. If you have sufficiently answered these questions in the word count you've been allotted, it's time to stop researching.

BREAK THIS RULE

Don't trust the web.

Back when writers took their first steps onto the Information Highway, this rule was practically hammered into their heads. This rule made plenty of sense...*then*. A lot of crap got posted and taken for gospel, and yes, crap still gets posted. But we do believe that the quality of reputable information you can find online has improved dramatically.

The internet has made the lives of freelancers much easier, and it should get the credit it deserves. As long as you double-check the information you find, read with a critical eye, and stick with reputable sites, you should be fine. In short, be a diligent, conscientious, and skeptical reporter.

What kinds of sites will give you a good start on research?

Google.

What would we do if we couldn't Google? This is the best search engine on the web because it indexes more web pages and returns more relevant results than other engines.

Federal, state, and local governments.

You can find which U.S. city has the highest number of violent crimes in a certain year, download economic reports, or check out the State Department's warnings about foreign travel.

Colleges and universities.

Larger universities have online access to library holdings, directories of their top experts, and research studies to peruse.

Major corporations.

If you're looking for financial information about a publicly held company, the SEC is monitoring them, so the information you find should be accurate.

Major media, print and broadcast.

Places like *The New York Times*, *The Wall Street Journal*, The Guardian, PBS, and more. Also web portals for trade-specific media like *Publishers Weekly*, *Advertising Age*, *Nation's Restaurant News*, *Financial Times*, and more.

RENEGADE RULE-BREAKER

Don Vaughan

Don Vaughan has been a full-time freelancer for 25 years. He's the founder of Triangle Association of Freelancers (TAF), which is among the largest organizations in North Carolina exclusively for nonfiction freelance writers. Read more about Don and his work at www.donaldvaughan.com.

How did you get started as a freelance writer?

I'd been freelancing since the early 1980s while working as a staff writer and then editor at various publications. I was working as an editor at the *National Examiner*, a tabloid newspaper, when I got a new boss who believed in management by terrorism. I was miserable and don't work well in that kind of stressful environment, so my wife Nanette suggested I quit to freelance. She had a good job, and by the time I left in September 1991, I had $3,000 in assignments lined up. Freelancing was something I desperately wanted to do but still, it was difficult making that leap—it was like jumping into a swimming pool at night and hoping there was water in there!

What is your biggest challenge today as a freelancer?

My biggest challenge has remained a constant throughout my career, which is generating work. I write for a lot of magazines regularly and editors often reach out to me with assignments, and that's great. But I still spend a lot of time pitching ideas and looking for new markets for my work. The industry has changed a lot. For example, I used to do bigger articles for more money, but today, articles are shorter, which means lower word counts. Today I may have a lot of work, but I'm always wondering what tomorrow will bring.

What do you wish you knew about freelancing when you started out?

First, I love freelancing and don't ever want to do anything else, but it can be a stressful job. I've often got tight deadlines and sources aren't getting back to me, or sometimes an article won't come together so I've got to tear it apart and start over again. I know I have a dream job—I can work at home, make my own hours—but there is a certain amount of stress I didn't expect in the beginning.

The second thing I wish I knew was the importance of casting a wide net. I learned a hard lesson after 9/11. Magazine advertising dried up, so editorial pages shrunk and assignments dropped off. It got so bad that I ended up taking a job at Borders for a short time. Luckily work picked up, but the experience taught me a valuable lesson, that I need to write for as many markets as I can and to keep my options open. It's why today, even though I'm busy with ongoing work, I'm always reaching out to new markets and editors.

What writing or business "rules" have you broken during your freelancing career?

I tend to be a rule follower, but the one rule I've broken in my career is cold-calling editors. Sometimes I want a quick yes or no, and it's easier to pick up the phone to get it. It hasn't always resulted in work, but those answers do save me time. I have a huge goal of writing for *Rolling Stone*; I've been pitching them for years. So one day I had an idea and I thought, "To heck with it, I'm going to call them." I got the managing editor on the line, pitched my story, and he asked me to send a proposal.

Though they didn't buy my story, it was a good experience for me. You're not going to get in trouble if you pitch over the phone to an editor; they'll listen as long as you don't harass them or take up too much of their time. If you can make a good case in two minutes, it's worth that call.

What advice would you give to a writer who's struggling as a freelancer?

Being a professional is vitally important. Here's what that means: You approach your assignments with a good attitude. You adhere to deadlines and word counts. You deliver a good story, but understand you will probably be asked to revise and you *will* be edited—that's part of the job, your obligation to the editor. Experienced writers know a skilled editor will make their writing better. Your goal should be to make an editor's job easier, not harder. You want to be the writer who doesn't need hand-holding.

I'm a strong advocate of not writing for free. I understand some writers do it at the beginning of their careers to get a byline, but once you've got that clip, it's time to find markets that will pay. If an editor is being paid, there's money there for the writer, too. If not money, then a subscription, merchandise, something tangible for the effort. If your writing is good enough to be printed, it's good enough to be compensated.

If you want to become a better writer, read writers who write outstanding nonfiction. I tell my students to read *Esquire* and *GQ*, which consistently run some of the best magazine nonfiction out there. Bylines I look for include Tom Chiarella, Tom Junod, John H. Richardson, Sean Flynn, A.J. Jacobs, and Scott Raab. And don't forget those classic nonfiction masters like John McPhee and Gay Talese.

As your career advances, don't become complacent. Pitch upward to higher-tier magazines so you can be ready for tomorrow. Success comes with perseverance. My career is proof.

CHAPTER 6

Talking the Talk: Renegade Interviewers Get the Story, and Then Some

Here are the rules: First you have to rack your brain formulating the perfect interview questions, then you have to wrangle good quotes out of your source, and then you have to spend hours transcribing your interview audio files. Yeah, right—if this were all true, we'd have quit long ago. Read on for the secrets to getting the most out of your interviews without going bonkers in the process.

BREAK THIS RULE

Write up your questions ahead of time and stick to them.

Having a list of questions that you need answered during an interview is a good idea, but remember that your questions are more like the signposts along the journey, not the road map. Sometimes you can get so wedded to your list that you don't bother to listen to what your source is telling you; you're in a hurry to move on to the next question. Other times the interviewee doesn't understand something you've asked, and you let the question slide, figuring you'll come back to it later. Most importantly, sticking rigidly to your list prevents you from asking better questions that may come up during your interview—answers to which may give your article more spark.

If you get queasy during interviews or you're a new freelancer, a prepared list of questions can reduce anxiety, especially if you know what information you specifically need from a source.

Diana, for example, runs through the same basic questions for all of her interviews, which not only is practical, but it does double-duty of easing all involved into the conversation. She asks the person to spell his name and give his proper job title, and she double-checks contact information. She created a checklist to make sure she gets this info right away. If certain facts must be confirmed by the source, she'll write those down, too. Once those are out of the way, she asks an overview question about the subject that naturally leads to the next question. The interviews always feel relaxed as a result.

Don't send your questions to the source ahead of time.

Some writers think if you send your questions to the source, you'll hear nothing but rehearsed, canned responses, but this has never been the case in our experience. Sending a list of questions lets the source prepare for the interview and ensures you'll get well-thought-out answers. We don't send every question we might possibly ask, but we do make sure the big, important questions are seen first. For example, while working on an article on food-borne illnesses for *Oxygen*, Linda sent the following list of questions to her sources:

1. Which foods have been the worst culprits in spreading food-borne illnesses?
2. How do foods get infected on the field, during processing, at the market, and in the home?
3. Is the situation in the U.S. getting better or worse?
4. What's being done by the government to protect consumers against food-borne illnesses?
5. What can consumers do to protect themselves?

Of course, this is a huge topic and Linda could have asked dozens of other questions—but these were essential for her article, and they were enough to give the sources an idea of what she was looking for. During the actual interviews, Linda asked additional questions targeted to her sources' areas of expertise.

If you're doing an investigative story, sending questions ahead of time may be tricky, especially if you have a wily source. In that case, you can provide her with an overview of what you'll be talking about so she can prepare.

BREAK THIS RULE

Formulate your own interview questions.

Many freelance writers carry this crazy notion in their head that they have to do everything for themselves: find their sources, figure out what questions to ask, and then conduct the interview. Why not do what one writer we know does? When he's discussing an assignment over the phone with his editor, he'll ask, "What questions do you want answered in this article?" Usually, his editor will come up a handful of great questions, which the writer then asks his sources.

If you're profiling someone, whether she's famous or unknown beyond her industry, ask a friend, family member, or colleague, "What would you like to know about this person?" The same question can be retooled for a travel article ("What would you want to know if you were planning a bike trip to Nova Scotia?") or even a service piece ("What would you consider a huge etiquette faux pas in the workplace?").

Another trick is to ask your source at the end of an interview, "Is there a question that you thought I would ask but haven't?" You'll get some interesting responses. One of Diana's cheekier sources answered, "Yeah, I thought you were going to ask me out." Obviously he didn't hear Diana's husband in the background.

Hate interviewing by phone? Interview your sources via email instead!

This is a "rule" we hear over and over not from true journalism experts or teachers, but from professional writers: "Hey, you hate interviews? Me too! Do what I do and email your questions to people!"

We know—phone interviews can be scary. Linda *still* experiences a tiny twinge of anxiety before each one! Some writers will argue that email interviews are fine. You ask questions, the source answers them. Done! Email interviews also have the advantage of giving the source a chance to really think about her answers, these writers say. And what if your source is overseas? Email is a painless way to snag interviews with people in other countries.

But taking the easy way out by doing email interviews is sloppy journalism. Unless you really, really can't get a key source to agree to an interview any other way, or your editor gives you explicit permission to interview your source over email, we strongly advise against this practice. (And the operative word here is "key"—if the source isn't absolutely essential to your article, you can find someone who *is* willing to talk on the phone.) Here's why.

1. You get canned answers.

The benefit of phone (or in-person) interviews is that you see the source as he really is and get unfiltered answers to your questions. Sometimes, the answers to questions you *didn't* ask make the best quotes. But with an email interview, you're basically giving the source permission to spin his own answers—and you often end up with canned, sanitized writing, which makes for terrible quotes. Not good.

2. You waste time.

Writers often think they'll save time if they shoot off their questions then sit back and wait for the answers. But the benefit of phone interviews is that if questions that aren't on your list come up as you do the interview—which they will—you can ask them right then. With an email interview, you have to email the source each time a new question comes up, and wait for the source to reply to each one, resulting in a time-consuming back-and-forth that's less likely to get all your questions answered. And if you're really lazy, you may put off the back-and-forth, thus jeopardizing the quality of your article.

3. Email interviews are easy to put off.

Linda used to do email interviews occasionally before she wised up, and one major drawback is that sources don't treat them as seriously as phone interviews. With a phone interview, you set a date and time and (usually) the source is there when you call. With an email interview, you send your questions and even if you give a deadline for responses, chances are you'll get the answers back only after days of nudging the source, which means you risk rushing at the last minute or even missing your deadline.

4. Many editors don't like them.

If you actually ask your editor whether she'll accept an email interview, she'll probably agree to one only if it's a key source and he refuses to speak on the phone. And don't think you can adopt a "don't ask, don't tell" policy: Technically, when you quote from an email interview you're supposed to append the quote with "said Jones in an email interview." That means if you do it right, you'll be outed as someone too lazy to do proper reporting.

5. There are no excuses.

"What if my source is overseas?" you may ask. To that we say, there are many ways around this. For example, Skype is often an option; we've interviewed sources in Norway, England, Italy, Taiwan, and Thailand via Skype. If the source doesn't use Skype, or any similar free calling platform, you can ask the editor if the publication will cover phone expenses, so you don't have to shell out for an international call. And if all else fails, consider it a cost of doing business and deduct the expense from your taxes. (You *are* earning enough from this assignment to make a $10 call worth it, right?)

6. You're essentially asking your sources to write your story for you and you're demanding a heck of a lot of *their* time to save *you* time, which is both lazy *and* rude.

Both Linda and Diana have been approached by writers wanting interviews, but instead of asking to schedule an interview, these writers have gone ahead, sent us anywhere from five to 12 questions, and requested that we write out our answers for them. To top it off, these are not "yes" or "no" answers; we've gotten questions like, "Tell me how you got started as a freelancing," "What are the three biggest mistakes newer writers make and give me tips how these mistakes can be overcome?" and "What are some of the psychological reasons behind gaining weight?" To which we want to answer: Are you flipping serious?

Writing out the answers to these questions could take us hours, especially because we're professional writers and you can bet your bottom we want to get our words right. A phone interview takes less time and effort for the source and yes, is more work for the writer but that's part of the job. In any case, Diana refuses to do email interviews, either as the writer or the source, and Linda requests email interviews only when she's looking for straight facts; for example, for a column she wrote about writers' conferences, she needed to know only basic details like the dates, price, and so on for each conference.

Don't fret if you hate phone interviews. Below, we have tips that will make interviews easier and less scary. Also keep in mind that the more interviews you do, the more comfortable you'll become picking up the phone.

BREAK THIS RULE

Don't do face-to-face interviews because they take up too much valuable time.

When Diana was a feature writer for a local chain of papers and new to the whole freelancing game, she met nearly every one of her sources in person to interview them. Most of the time the interviewees stuck to the time Diana allotted for them and she scored great visual details that added to her stories. For example, once she was interviewing the director of a local weight loss clinic when a couple came in for their weekly appointment. The couple agreed to share their story, and luckily, the newspaper's photographer arrived in time to capture their weigh-in.

Diana knows a more experienced writer who pooh-poohs face-to-face meetings because "they gobble up too much time." This writer insists on telephone or email interviews, period. True, a lot of interviews can be handled by phone (see above for why we don't recommend email interviews), but other stories require a more personal touch.

Pick up any newsstand magazine and figure out which writer interviewed the celebrity in person and which writer interviewed the celebrity over the phone. Sometimes the writer has no choice, especially when he's working with celebrities and their attendant handlers. For example, Linda used to interview celebs for *WebMD* magazine, and her editor would work with the celebrity's agent to set up a phone call. But stories that describe how a starlet hid her bloodshot eyes behind shades during a lunch interview at an LA hotspot are more interesting than ones that merely report what the starlet said about her latest movie.

And if you're interested in literary journalism, do you think for a moment that John McPhee interviewed geologists and orange farmers from the comfort of his home office? Or that Sebastian Junger didn't hang out in Gloucester, Massachusetts, to absorb the feel of the fishing community he was writing about? They probably had nice expense accounts, but still—if this is the kind of writing you want to do, you'll need to leave the house and get your hands dirty.

Most of our interviews are conducted by phone because that's what our stories require. If you're writing a service article for *Woman's Day* on how to clean a house in an hour, it makes little sense to meet your sources in person. But an in-depth profile of a local company with an innovative product? We'd go for the face-to-face time. Think about what your story requires to be the best it can be, and forget the rules that keep you tethered to your phone.

BREAK THIS RULE

Always transcribe your interview audio files.

Linda usually records her interviews, but she learned early on that if she's working on several meaty assignments at once, transcribing interviews eats up precious time. Ask yourself whether the interview is important enough to record, and if it is, whether you need to have every word in hard copy.

In certain cases we feel it's worth having a complete interview transcript, such as when we're speaking to someone about a controversial subject or the interviewee is giving us complex and vital information that may confuse us if we only take notes. Other times, we record and make notes while we're talking, then go back and transcribe only the important parts of the interview. After all, no law says the whole interview has to be transcribed. (There are, however, very strict laws about recording phone calls, so check your state's regulations before you go crazy with your recorder.)

If you decide you want a full transcript but don't have the time, pay someone else to do it. Linda's been using a professional transcription service for the last several years. It's well worth the $20 to $30 per interview to avoid the hassle of transcribing, especially since the articles typically pay from $400 to $2,500. And Diana once interviewed a couple of local professional transcriptionists and hired the best of the lot to transcribe hours of interviews she needed for a time-consuming investigative feature. Once she delegated this task, she felt energized to work on other parts of the project. Was it worth the cost? Absolutely, when you consider she then freed up her time to do the things she's good at doing, like finding more work.

If you're a crack typist, however, you can do what Eric does: He types his interviewees' answers right into his computer during the interview. He captures about 75 percent of the conversation, making sure he gets all the important information and leaving out repetitions, asides, and so on. He makes up abbreviations on the fly and goes back to fill in missing information once the interview ends. You can even buy apps, like TextExpander, that will automatically expand any abbreviation you define.

People love to talk about themselves.

Too many writers, wanting to come off as seasoned professionals, launch right into their interview questions. But if you corner an interview subject and begin firing away, he can shut down, especially if he's shown any reluctance to speak with you in the first place. Getting great quotes from "hot" sources can be difficult, but getting them from someone who's lukewarm takes a tremendous amount of skill, patience, and often outright cunning.

For a job trend story for an IT magazine, one of Diana's regular sources put her in contact with a software programmer he talked up as "the dream job candidate," someone who'd be perfect to interview for this story. This programmer was brilliant, tops in his field, and the recruiter was sure this guy would have great stories to share about his work life.

This source may have been a "dream job candidate," but he was a limp noodle as an interviewee. For starters, he had a thick accent that was hard to understand. Diana's attempts to warm him up with her brief comedy routine at the beginning of the interview were greeted with silence. While sweat trickled down Diana's back, the programmer figured out how to answer every one of her open-ended questions with a monotone "Yes" or "No."

Afterwards, Diana reviewed her notes and listened to the recorded monologue, and found not a single good quote to use in this story. Nothing. Zilch. So she emailed the programmer a couple of "I'll need some clarification" questions. This time, he added a few new answers to his standard retinue of "Yes" and "No": some compelling "Maybes" and a couple gripping "I don't knows." Still not one quote to be found. Diana reclaimed the interview by writing about the source in the third person, and then asking a job recruiter to comment on this programmer's skill set.

Interviewing someone who's tongue-tied can drive a writer to panic, but the little tricks below can improve or salvage the experience.

Perfect your lead-in.

Many times you're so eager to bag your prey that you forget to lure them into your camp. It's important to spend a little time courting your source because then you can assess whether you'll need two pens to keep up with him, or you'll need to whip out advanced tricks to get him to talk. Your lead-in can be businesslike ("Thanks for speaking with me today, John. I need your expertise for this article I'm writing for *Business Monthly* about credit card fraud.") or frightfully mundane ("So, how's the weather in Chicago?"). Think of it as dinner party chit chat, but you only have to do it for a minute.

Tell them what you want.

We're not advising you to make up quotes and attribute them to your tight-lipped sources. But it helps to remember that your interviewee usually isn't privy to the big picture of your story. If you can explain how she fits into your piece ("I need a few quotes from a security expert about how homeowners can protect their valuables"), this may be enough to relax her. When Diana worked as a marketing communications manager for a packaged goods company, reporters from trade publications often contacted her to talk about her industry's packaging issues. It was disconcerting when a reporter peppered her with questions without explaining the piece he was working on. Was it an exposé on the tactics marketers use to sell products? Or was it a roundup about the challenges marketers face when they sell their products overseas?

Get it in writing.

While we generally advise against email interviews (see "BREAK THIS RULE: Formulate your own interview questions"), if you have a *key* source who is a dud on the phone, ask your editor's permission to interview him via email. Certain people do much better with email interviews. People who choke up on the phone sometimes turn into great quotesmiths on paper (like writers, for example). Email interviews are also attractive to some sources because they can answer the questions at their leisure and take the time to come up with the perfect replies.

Forget the word "interview."

Refer to the interrogation as a "conversation," a "talk," or a "chat"—anything but an interview—and that may be enough to thaw a nervous source. In fact, if this is a really important interview for you, try to spend as much time with your source as you can doing anything but interviewing. Then, when she's relaxed, ask her a few easy questions. Then go back to the chit chat. You'll notice that some of the well-known network interviewers do this: Diane Sawyer often looks like she's best friends with her subject, until she moves closer and asks her, "Now, Sue, tell me...did you murder your husband?"

Feel their pain. Share a little.

When Diana interviewed women who had been dealing with physically and emotionally painful fertility problems for a potential story, she let them know that she, too, had run the gauntlet of reproductive issues. It helped these women to know they were speaking with someone who understood what they were going through.

When all else fails, tell them exactly what you want.

If you're paying attention, you'll notice we mentioned something like this a couple of bullet points ago. Only now we add the word *exactly*. When you've got a source who simply can't give good quote, it's okay help him out. Think of what you would like him to say, and then start this out with "Would you agree that...?" or "Is it accurate to say...?" Your source's words can be salvaged by summarizing his quote, like this: "Jones agrees that Dr. Smith's latest diet book is filled with nutritional misinformation." Or the opposite if he doesn't agree. You don't actually have to quote him, unless your editor is adamant about having copy between quotation marks.

BREAK THIS RULE

Don't let the interview veer off course.

One of the most rewarding aspects of a freelance writing career is talking to interesting people. Sure, a lot of times your interviews are rote, but now and then you'll find someone who gives you a million ideas for new stories. If you're married to a list of questions or have set a strict time limit for the interview, you can miss these opportunities without even realizing it.

Here's an example of why flexibility is so important:

Diana was looking for a local business that used offshore software programmers on IT projects, so she sent an email to her source network for help. One of her contacts happened to have read a newspaper article about a business like this, so she sent Diana the company name. Diana called and explained to the business owner what she was looking for, and the man invited her to his office since it was in the next town over.

That interview was one of the most profitable hours Diana has ever spent with a source. Although the article's focus wasn't putting this source's business in the best light with her target audience (American information technology workers who were losing jobs to offshore workers), her source was still willing to share his controversial position with these readers.

What was more interesting was that this source was from China, and he was pursuing the American dream with glee. His enthusiasm for his business was infectious. He had created unique software tools to enable his employees in China to work closely with clients in the U.S. He had recently become a U.S. citizen and was proud of what he had achieved in his adopted country.

Over the next several months, Diana came back to this interview to sell more stories. A sister publication of the one she originally wrote for wanted a cover story on the overseas software development market. Her source had given her an excellent overview, so she added another $2,500 to her pocket. Ka-ching! Then she pitched and sold a story to a website about how companies with offices in different time zones improve communications. Ka-ching! Next was a piece on web-based offshore software development. Ka-ching! Another $2,000 in the coffers. Diana was nowhere near exhausting the well of information this source opened up for her. In less than six months she'd earned over $6,000 from one interview.

Freelancer Bethanne Kelly Patrick also lets her interviews "flow" and often turns up interesting new angles to her stories, or new stories altogether. For example, one day she was talking to a publishing executive about new book titles, and he mentioned author Carl Hiaasen. She happened to be a Hiaasen fan, and their conversation led Patrick to write a short piece about the quirky author's friendship with musician Warren Zevon.

So don't be afraid to let the interview wander off course. Train your ear for information that might give your article a different spin, or perhaps even spur a proposal for a totally different story. If the interview is interesting and you both have time to spare, feel free to let the conversation take on a life of its own. You never know where it will lead you.

But what about the "rule" that keeping interviews short is more efficient, both time-wise and money-wise? Tell your source ahead of time that you've scheduled X minutes for the interview. If he's one of those sources who tends to ramble, you can blame the time constraints when you ask him to get back on track, and alert him when you're close to your selected end time (more on this below). If you find he's a delightful interview, you can conveniently "forget" to remind him that your allotted time is almost up.

BREAK THIS RULE

Don't interrupt the interviewee.

Ah, yes, the runaway interview where your source is rambling on and on about his great-grandmother Billings—or was it his great- grandmother Michaels?—whose pole beans won not one, not two, but three blue ribbons at the Iowa State Fair. And before you can interject a question that brings the interview back on track, he's off and running about how you should write an article on the inequities of State Fair judging.

We've been there. We feel your pain. We've suffered through too many of these interviews and we've learned that in these cases, damn the etiquette books—it's okay to cut these talkative folks off at the first utterance of "May I digress?" No, they may not and yes, we're advising interviewus interruptus. Sure, we said above that you should be open to letting the interview veer off course, but only you can tell whether that off-course rambling will net you more ideas versus waste your energy.

If it's the latter, do we even need to point out what a huge waste of time and money this is for you? If you're recording and transcribing the interview, you're going to have to listen to this person drone on yet again to get the interesting bits you managed to wrangle from the interview. If you're paying someone to do your transcriptions, you'll be doubly annoyed when you receive twelve pages of useless dialog with a hefty transcription bill.

Something else to consider if you're shy about dealing with a motormouth: how to handle the fallout after the article appears. In our experience these loquacious sources are not shy about picking up the phone to complain about the scanty coverage you gave them in your article after they spent so long talking with you. This means another time-wasting intervention with this source. Do you want to listen to him all over again, only this time with his serious attitude problem?

Diana has found that a bit of interview prep can help: First, she usually tells her interviewees prior to the interview what questions she needs answered so they arrive at the conversation with a goal in mind (see "BREAK THIS RULE: Don't send your questions to the source ahead of time"). Another trick she learned from her job as a marketing manager is to set a time limit for the interview. You can do this two ways: you can hammer it into your source a couple of times that this a 10-, 15-, or 30-minute interview, or you can fib a bit and tell him you have another appointment that follows. This may feel like a lie to you, but is it really? Your source doesn't need to know your next appointment is with a grilled cheese sandwich, tomato soup, and Netflix.

Speaking of honesty, a bit of that can help, especially when sprinkled with a liberal amount of flattery. Diana often tells her more verbose interviewees that as much as she'd love to chat all afternoon because they're so interesting (the flattery), this assignment has a word limit (the truth) and she doesn't want to waste their valuable time (more flattery) only to get one quote (more honesty). This usually brings interviewees back on track.

BREAK THIS RULE

Offer a verbal "thank you" to your sources and move on.

Of course you should thank your sources when you're winding up interviews, but that's not all you should do. Many writers send written thank-yous to their sources. It takes only a minute to jot down a quick note, and written thank-you notes from a writer are so rare that sources will definitely remember you kindly when you need to interrupt their busy schedules again in the future. You can also drop your business card into the note. Who knows...maybe the source will pass it along to a friend who needs a writer!

And for sources who go above and beyond the call of duty to help you with an article, a small gift may be in order. Linda once had a source she called again and again for nutrition articles. When this nutritionist spent several hours of her vacation putting together a six-day sugar-free diet, Linda was so grateful she sent her a basket of handmade soaps.

This isn't to say you should ever pay or bribe sources. If a source asks to be compensated for his time, head the other way. Paying sources brings up an ethical dilemma: You want an unbiased opinion, but a source who's being paid is likely to tell you only what you want to hear. We also don't accept gifts from our sources, apart from review copies of their books, though we know of many ethical, conscientious colleagues who will accept a box of chocolates around the holidays. However, we see no harm in sending a small, inexpensive token of thanks to sources who regularly share their expertise with you.

BREAK THIS RULE

You have to do your own interviews.

This seems to go without saying: You got the gig, you do the interviews. However, if you're too busy to interview—or it's not a core competency for you—and you can afford it, hiring an interviewer can give you more time for doing what you're best at, not to mention landing more assignments. (A caveat: If you decide to go this route, check your assignment contracts first. Some contracts stipulate that you don't outsource any part of the assignment.)

During a period when Linda had more assignments than time, she hired another writer to conduct interviews for her. Linda would find the source and write up the questions, and the other writer would set and conduct the interview and send Linda the transcript. The writer she hired was an excellent interviewer. Linda got more work done, the interviewer made some extra cash, and Linda's editors received well-written, on-time articles. Everyone was happy.

If you're overloaded with work and think you'd like to hire someone to handle your interviews, your best bet may be to hire a magazine or newspaper writer who's looking to make a few extra bucks. You can find likely candidates by keeping an eye on forums and email discussion groups that cater to writers, advertising in places like Craigslist, or searching for writers on sites like Fiverr. Pay your interviewer what she's worth, and you'll both come out on top.

RENEGADE RULE-BREAKER

Kelly James

Kelly James is the author of *Six-Figure Freelancing: The Writer's Guide to Making More Money.*

How did you get started as a freelance magazine writer?

I actually started writing and selling articles when I was still working full time as a lawyer. I sold my first two articles to *Cosmopolitan* and *Bride's* and started thinking, "Gee, maybe I could do this full time." And the truth is that after five and a half years of practicing, I really wanted to escape the law. I saved enough to live on for six months while I launched my full-time freelance career January 1, 1997.

What was the biggest challenge you faced, and how did you overcome it?

For me, it was the radical transition from being constantly surrounded by people to working alone. (Well, except for my golden retriever, who probably saved my sanity.) It was a big shock going from dealing with clients, appearing in court, and having meetings all day to the quiet and isolation of laboring in my home office. I missed the human contact, but I eventually got used to it—and found ways to incorporate more of it into my workday with lunches with friends, going to the gym, etc. More than 19 years later, I actually prefer working alone—I think I've discovered (and embraced!) my inner introvert.

What would you say is the most important piece of advice you can give a fledgling writer?

Know the market you're pitching to. The timeliest, most well-researched, most intriguing query won't do you any good if it's not a good fit for the magazine. Yet a lot of writers focus more on the ideas *they* want to write rather than on the ideas an editor is likely to buy. If you're pitching a content company, the same advice goes—know what types of clients they work for, and what industries they work in. Knowledge helps set you apart from your competitors.

Did you learn any new tips yourself as you were writing *Six-Figure Freelancing*?

I updated *Six-Figure Freelancing* several years after I published the first edition and I learned a lot, actually. I interviewed more than 20 successful six-figure writers for each edition of the book. I think the point that really resonated with me was how versatile and adaptable successful writers are—and have to be, especially today! Most of the writers I interviewed have been full-time freelancers for more than a decade, and over the years, all have expanded and changed the foci of their businesses, whether by learning new skills, covering new subjects, expanding into different areas, making the transition from magazines to books, or transitioning from magazines to corporate writing.

The key is to adapt and roll with the market—know what clients want and be able to deliver. As I write this in 2016, for many writers, that means producing content for a variety of clients, something that wasn't even on my radar when I started freelancing almost two decades ago.

What's the most renegade thing you've done in your writing career?

That's an easy one—I was a renegade from day one! I wrote an article and sent it in instead of querying, and on top of that, I sent it to a national market. And it sold! (That was "Surviving your Last Two Weeks on the Job" for *Cosmo*.) I did the same thing with my second sale to *Bride's*. Not the most efficient way of working, and I don't recommend it for new writers, but it did work for me. I suppose sometimes ignorance really is bliss.

Is there anything else you'd like to add?

One of the things I suggest when I teach magazine writing is to look for markets that you can write for more than once. It's much easier to get more work from an editor who already knows you than to continually scout for new markets. You have to continually market yourself as a magazine freelancer, but it's nice to have a stable of "regulars," especially when editors start coming to you with assignments. The same is true with content clients. At this point in my career, about 80 percent of my shorter work (articles, online writing, blog posts) comes from regular clients and more than 90 percent of my ghostwriting work (books and proposals) comes through word-of-mouth recommendations. The less time I spend pitching, the more time I have to write—and that helps me hit the six-figure mark.

That's why I think it's important that all writers focus on building relationships, not just on getting assignments. For more info, visit my website at www.becomebodywise.com.

It's been ten years since you spoke to us. How has your career changed?

As far as what's different now than ten years ago, 80-90 percent of my work now is ghostwriting books and book proposals for clients; the rest of my work is content, primarily for content companies and a few stand-alone publications as well. I still do some speaking as well. I got into books about 15 years ago but quickly found it was more lucrative to coauthor and ghostwrite books for clients instead of writing my own. (In fact, I wrote a book about that subject for freelancers as well: *Goodbye Byline, Hello Big Bucks, Second Edition: Make Money Ghostwriting Books, Articles, Blogs and More.*) My goal, as always, is to make a full-time living in part-time hours, and a mix of ghosting and content writing is helping me do that.

Putting Pen to Paper: The Rights and Wrongs of Writing

The grammar rules we break in this chapter would make your eighth-grade English teacher faint. And if that isn't incentive enough to read this chapter, we also tell you how to write about your sex life without your mother finding out, how to get free fact checking for your articles, and when it can be okay to miss your deadline.

BREAK THIS RULE

Begin writing when you have all your info.

Among the slang of the magazine world—nut graf, on spec, lede—is the expression "TK," which stands for "tokum," an intentional misspelling of "to come." Why misspell it, you ask? Because "to come" is common enough phrasing to appear in copy, whereas "tokum" is not, which makes it easier to do a search and destroy mission on it before the final proofing. Writers and editors use TK to stand in for missing information that will be added later. A writer might send off a query with the title "TK Ways to Write Without All Your Information," for example, and the number that replaces TK will be solidified once the writer has a firm word count from the editor.

When you're writing an article and need a stat or compelling quote, don't drop everything to search for the perfect bit of info—drop a TK in the hole and keep writing so you don't break your flow of concentration.

"I frequently begin to write before I have much at all," says freelance writer Leslie Pepper. She gets her rough thoughts down on paper, adding an all-caps TK HERE whenever needed, then finds experts to fill those gaps without conducting more general interviews. "It makes researching much more streamlined," she says. "Why bother with extraneous info?" Do double-check, though, that all your TKs are filled before turning in the article!

BREAK THIS RULE

Write your article long before the due date.

Alas, many of us work better with some flames toasting our buns. Our advice is to work within your own comfort level. Diana and Linda research and interview weeks before deadline, but save the actual writing until a few days before D-day. Another writer we know has interviewed for and written 3,000-word articles on the day they're due. She does a damn good job of it, too as her previous job as a newspaper writer perfected her super-sleuthing skills and taught her to write tight and fast.

You don't need to beat a deadline by weeks or even by days—your editor likely won't even look at the article until after the deadline anyway. That said, you may want to give yourself at least a few days to write the article so you can put it aside for a day or so, then examine it with a fresh eye while doing the final edit. You can catch a lot of bloopers that way.

When Linda was starting out, she always gave herself three days to write an article once she finished the research. On day one, she wrote half the article. On day two, she wrote the second half. And on day three, she printed it out and went over the whole thing with a red pen, repeating this process several times until she was happy with the piece. She then had Eric give the article a going-over. The day before the deadline, Linda printed out the article one final time to check for overlooked mistakes before turning it in.

Now that she has more experience, Linda has streamlined the process—not printing out the article so many times, for example, and not running it by her husband (unless she's having trouble with the piece)— but she still gives herself two days to write a piece, and she turns it in the day before the deadline whenever possible.

If an editor gives you an assignment topic, assume it's a good story.

Sometimes it seems editors have nothing better to do than brainstorm pre-posterous, undoable ideas and fob them off on writers. An idea that sounds good in email doesn't always work out in real life. Almost every writer can tell a horror story about the article topic that wouldn't die. Here for your perusing is one such tale, which we call Systems for Billing, Systems Worth Killing.

Once upon a time, the editor of a utilities trade mag asked Linda to find industry analysts who would compare and grade different types of online billing systems. The premise seemed friendly and inviting, but it soon revealed a few hidden thorns. First of all, none of the analysts—some of who represented the systems to be compared—wanted to stick their necks out by grading products. Second, the billing systems came in so many different formats that comparisons were meaningless, something the analysts repeatedly told Linda.

Linda contacted the editor three weeks before the deadline to let him know that the analysts refused to compare systems that couldn't even be compared, and she begged him to put a stake in that topic and kill it. The editor instead suggested she contact more analysts. She did, and after another week, Linda again called the editor to tell him the topic wasn't working. The new analysts wouldn't talk either, and they insisted that comparing these products made no sense.

But the topic refused to die! Or rather the editor refused to kill it, again encouraging Linda to speak to more analysts.

Desperate, she wrote to several writers' email discussion lists, begging for help. The writers sympathized, but had no solutions for offing this particular zombie topic.

The deadline arrived, and Linda still had no article. The editor shouldn't have been surprised since Linda had warned him for weeks that this topic couldn't be cornered, but he was furious; it turns out the deadline fell on his final day on the job, and now he would have to spend extra time at work to write the article himself. No wonder he kept urging Linda to keep at it! Linda never landed another assignment from that magazine, and as far as she knows, the article topic never appeared and is still stumbling around the wildlands of one editor's fevered mind. The End.

Tales of zombie topics don't have to end in disaster; sometimes a change in slant is all you need to solve the problem of the impossible article. In one instance, Linda was assigned an article on how small business owners can follow their business plan. Hundreds of books are dedicated to this topic, but the editor wanted it in 1,500 words. Linda spoke with a few experts and discovered a common theme: A business plan is always a work in progress, and sometimes it shouldn't be followed. With the editor's permission, Linda ended up writing the article about how and when to change your plan.

So if you feel a story isn't working out, let your editor know as soon as possible. Most editors will be willing to slant the idea differently, or even give you another idea that's more doable. And for those editors too pigheaded to understand that some topics can't be tamed? Hand them a proverbial crossbow, and invite them to hunt the topic themselves. Maybe then they'll learn to face reality.

BREAK THIS RULE

Never mess with a quote.

When we asked several editors and successful writers if they'd feel comfortable cleaning up their sources' quotes, we almost started a writer's war, complete with lobbed laptops and zinging paperclips. You'd have thought we'd asked them about cleaning up their sources' bathrooms.

"No. It is not [acceptable to change a quote]," says writer Judy Waytiuk. "If the quote needs cleaning up, keep the part that works, paraphrase the rest—accurately—and put in quotes only the direct quote material you've actually used."

That's the ideal, but it's an ideal that writers find hard to live up to. "I've tried to be good and quote 100 percent. But there's a problem with this because normal speech doesn't lend itself to written text very well," says writer Maggie Bonham. "What you end up doing is making your source look like an idiot. What's better is to put the quote in coherent sentences and not change the context. Make them look smart and like experts and you'll never get a complaint." Bonham may have something there, judging by how many sources have asked Linda and Diana to clean up the quotes and not make them "sound stupid" in print.

Elisa Bosley, editor-in-chief emeritus of *Delicious Living*, admits she tinkers. "I often change quotes slightly to get them to flow better or make grammatical sense," she says. "People rarely talk in neat, printable quotes. Just don't change the meaning in any way, and verify it with the person." If you need to make changes beyond cleaning up quotes, try paraphrasing the ideas instead of using direct quotes.

Yet in certain cases you *do* want to capture the unique speech patterns, the hesitancies, and the garbled grammar of your sources. Say you're writing a story on the sharp decline of student test scores in a certain school district, and your sources are pointing fingers at the new educational consultant who was hired shortly before the scores started to plummet. When you interview her, you find she can barely get a sentence out of her mouth without committing a humorous malapropism. In this case, would you clean up her quotes? She'd probably be happy to discover you'd changed "indecent" to "indigent" for her, but using her exact words would have more impact with the "indecent families" of her district.

BREAK THIS RULE

Don't write anything you wouldn't want your mother to see.

All too often our assignments—or our artistic sensibilities—require us to expose our foibles, rehash humiliating anecdotes about our friends and family, or reveal intimate details about our personal lives. How can we deal with the dilemma of writing for an audience of thousands on topics we wouldn't mention to our own mothers? How does a writer write about, say, his search for the perfect toupee, knowing friends and family will soon be privy to his hair-raising secret?

Lie.

Linda subscribes to this technique herself. When her mother-in-law asked what articles she was working on, no way was Linda about to tell her that she had finished a saucy article for *Redbook* called "The Better Orgasm Diet"; instead, she said she had written a piece on "nutrition."

Greg Blanchette is another writer who uses this approach. Blanchette undertook an ambitious sailing voyage around the world in a small, open boat, and wrote a series of articles about the trip for a sailing magazine. "My parents, of course, wanted copies of the articles," says Blanchette. "What makes a good article in a sailing mag is thrills, danger, narrow escapes—of which there were plenty. But that's not what a parent wants to read, so I assured them that the hairy parts were played up for dramatic effect. They weren't."

Protect the innocent.

You're reading an article about people with a shoe-sniffing fetish, and you notice that one of the names is marked with an asterisk. Your gaze drops to the bottom of the page, where it notes, "This name has been changed." Do you enjoy the article any less now that you know the fetish-ist's name has been changed? Of course not.

Before you try this tactic, check with your editor. *Redbook* was once interested in a slightly raunchy idea of Linda's, but the magazine required sources to use their real names. The result: Although Linda found plenty of anonymous anecdotes, she couldn't come up with a single person who wanted to talk about her bedroom romps on the record.

Fake your name.

By day, Jane Simons writes service pieces for family magazines. By night, she becomes Felicity West, a risqué writer who pens erotica for a living. Pen names are yet another tool for the wallflower writer. "My erot-ica writing might prove both embarrassing to my family and detrimental to my other writing projects, especially for the family magazines," says Simons. "Using a pen name allows me to write erotica, which pays fairly well, without compromising the rest of my assignments. I'm not ashamed of what I write, but I've seen other writers lose the bulk of their more le-gitimate writing assignments when it was discovered they wrote erotica."

The one drawback to using a pen name is that Simons can't take credit for her erotica on her writing résumé, "so it appears, at the moment, that I have no fiction writing credits." However, adds Simons, "I've received strange 'fan' mail, and I'm just as happy that those people can't easily find me."

Negotiate.

Have a frank discussion with your friends and family about what you want to write and what they feel comfortable with you disclosing. When Diana and her husband were honeymooning in Italy, her husband dropped a bomb on her: He wanted her to keep their personal lives personal: no articles about husbands who stole the covers or snored too loudly, or play-by-plays of their first date. Tears were shed, sharp words were exchanged, but over a couple of months they negotiated a compromise. Diana prom-ised that she would never mention her husband by name in any of her ar-ticles and that she'd continue writing under her maiden name. Her husband agreed to zip his lips when it came to subjects she wanted to write about.

BREAK THIS RULE

It's boring to use the same word all the time, so jazz up your writing with synonyms.

We know of a book that offers writers 150 synonyms for *said*, but we say, "No way." And we don't stutter it, blurt it, or twang it. We *say* it.

We use the verb *say* so much that we tend to gloss right over all the "he saids" and "she saids" when we read. The same goes for other words you may feel you're overusing in an article; for example, if you're writing a parenting piece you may be bored of writing the word *baby* and feel tempted to start replacing it with *munchkin, infant, tot,* and *little one* (a term one parenting mag editor we know despises). Of if you're working on a piece about cars, after a while you may feel the urge to crack open a thesaurus to find replacements like *auto, ride,* and *wheels*.

Once in awhile it's refreshing to use a different word, but constantly going out of your way to use different words in place of the simplest and most basic ones jolts the reader from the flow of the writing. Besides, you can't really "giggle" out a sentence, nor can you "anguish" or "sigh" it, unless you're the heroine of a badly written romance novel.

When Linda interned at a lifestyle magazine in San Francisco, she once edited an article by a writer who apparently had a phobia of the word "say." His sources all snorted, riffed, chuckled, and wheedled, and this made the writing sound amateurish and drew the reader's attention from what was actually being said. Linda doggedly edited the article, changing 99 percent of the writer's unique creations to the plain old boring word "said."

So don't worry that your readers will get sick of seeing the word *sugar* in an article about how to cut sugar from your diet, or the word *game* in an article about boardgames. They *expect* to see those words, so keep calm and write on.

BREAK THIS RULE

Use perfect grammar.

As a writer, you should know the rules of grammar. Even if you can't *explain* the rules, you often know in your bones when a verb is in the wrong tense or a word is used incorrectly. As you become more experienced, you'll learn that sometimes breaking grammar rules makes for stronger copy, especially when you're writing for the consumer magazine market or blogs, where articles are typically written in a friendly, off-the-cuff, grammatically imperfect style.

Many of the rules that were drummed into you in elementary school can be safely erased from your memory banks. "A whole bunch of rules were never historically a part of our language," says Howard Faulkner, Ph.D., an English and grammar professor emeritus at Washburn University in Topeka, Kansas. "When grammar books started being written in the 1700s, Latin was taken as the model. But Latin is a particularly bad model because it's a synthetic language, meaning it depends on word endings as opposed to word order as in English. So these early grammar books promulgated these 'rules,' and for some reason they keep coming down." For example:

Never split an infinitive.

In Latin, sure, a split infinitive is a no-no. English, on the other hand, still works fine and dandy with split infinitives.

"Instinctively, some things sound better with a certain word order," says freelance writer Maggie Bohnam, who has studied both Anglo-Saxon and Latin. "We know that the 'to' in the phrase 'to boldly go' (from *Star Trek*) works with the infinitive verb 'go.' If we were to correct the split infinitive, I don't think it would make that big of a clarification. Besides, 'To boldly go where no one has gone before' sounds so much better than

'To go boldly where no one has gone before.'" The bottom line: Write it both ways, then make a decision on your own as to which sounds best.

Never start a sentence with 'and' or 'but.'

"If you have a teacher who says this, bring a copy of the Bible into class—the King James version," says Faulkner. "I'm sure the teacher will say 'This is a masterpiece of literature.' Open it to any page at random, and you will find sentence after sentence beginning with 'and' or 'but.'"

Never end a sentence with a preposition.

Wrong. "It's perfectly normal and natural to end sentences with a preposition," says Faulkner.

Never use sentence fragments.

Beginning writers should follow this rule since sentence fragments, used improperly, can confuse the reader. But once you know what you're doing, fragment away! The second paragraph in one of Faulkner's books (Howard Faulkner, mind you) opens with the one word sentence "Shamefully." "It's meant to be grammatically effective," he says.

While fragments are fine, stay away from the unbelievably popular style of marketing speak that uses each word as an individual sentence, such as "Real. Food. Fast." We understand how this is meant to be interpreted, but it comes across as the labored wheezing of three-pack-a-day smoker.

In conclusion: Don't let the grammar books crush your voice or suck the juice out of your writing. Learn the rules, but remember that rules can be effectively broken in the hands of a skilled writer—and that some rules, like the ones above, aren't even rules at all.

BREAK THIS RULE

You have to hit the word count dead on.

Freelancer Judy Waytiuk is really on the ball. If she gets an assignment for 1,200 words, she hands in 1,200 words. On the dot. Even if she has to add or subtract an adjective or two. That's great if you can do it, but don't let word-count worries keep you awake at night.

We've heard it's usually okay to miss the word count by plus or minus ten percent, so if you have an assignment for 2,000 words, 1,800 to 2,200 words would technically be acceptable.

However, most editors we know would be disappointed, if not annoyed, if you handed in a piece that's 200 words too short. Over is always better than under, as it's easier for your editor to trim words than to add them. (Think of all those deleted scenes on DVDs and how much better the movie is without those scenes. They were removed for a reason!)

"Personally, I don't mind cutting up to 300 words," says Lisa Hannam, health editor at *Glow* magazine. "Sometimes when you're working on a piece, a second set of eyes really helps. Beyond 300 though, it's annoying. I trust that the writer knows and understands which information is more important in the article after researching the topic. But never, ever go under the word count. It means you haven't done enough research or the topic isn't worth the space assigned."

Naturally, if you're writing a 200-word short, we don't advise going 100-plus words over the limit. "I hate it when an article comes in at double the assigned word count," says Elisa Bosley, editor-in-chief emeritus of *Delicious Living*. "The writer isn't distilling the important information him- or herself, leaving me to do it instead."

Don't let the length constraint keep you from throwing in a few sidebars if the magazine runs them, though, even if they take you over the word count. If you have extra information from your research and can whip out a sidebar or two, your editor will love you even more than she already undoubtedly does.

BREAK THIS RULE

You should always turn your articles in on time.

Would your editor rather receive a timely article that's not quite there, or a great article that's a few days late? "Neither is good," says Jeremy White, editor of *Pizza Today*. "But a great article a day or two after deadline, provided the writer asked for an extension, is preferable to a sub-par article that will eventually take more time due to the need for rewriting or heavy editing. A sub-par article means the writer probably will not get another assignment. A great article that comes in late will get a new writer one more chance, but the next one better be on time."

Your deadline decision also depends on the situation. If your editor says she's in a rush and needs the piece by a certain date or else, you might make her look bad to her superiors if it isn't ready on time. Remember: One important duty of the freelance writer is to make editors' jobs easier, not extinct. Your delinquent article could even cause the publication to be late to the printer, or delay the posting process online, which won't endear you to anyone on staff. If you're having problems with an article and you can't get a deadline extension, do everything within your power to make your article perfect; pulling an all-nighter and asking writer friends for comments and suggestions are two ways to do this.

You'll probably get a feeling during your research and hunt for sources whether the assignment will be troublesome. If you have an inkling that you're not going to make the deadline, call your editor as soon as possible to ask for an extension rather than submit something that's on time but not your best work.

BREAK THIS RULE

Once you turn your article in, it's out of your hands.

Smart freelancers request to see the galley proofs—a copy of the edited and laid-out article—before the magazine goes to press. (With online markets, this could simply be your edited piece minus the layout.)

And for good reason. Linda once wrote an article about spring cleaning for a popular women's magazine, turned it in, and promptly forgot about it. What a nasty surprise she had when she saw the article in the magazine and discovered the editors had invented quotes for her sources! We're not talking slightly altered quotes—we're talking completely made-up facts and assertions.

Other mistakes that make it into print may be less galling than the example above but they're no less annoying. For example, when Diana got married, one of her editors mistakenly assumed she'd be using her married name for her byline. Another time, her family bought her Christmas presents based on something she "wrote" in a women's magazine article; unfortunately, they were the goodies her editor had inserted into the article.

In another case, Linda wrote a reported essay for a major health magazine, and when the fact checker called her to go over the details, Linda was surprised to learn she's 5' 4" (she's 5' 6") and addicted to Mexican food, one of her least favorite cuisines.

Linda learned her lesson and often asks to see galleys; the editor doesn't always agree, but when he does, Linda is occasionally able to fix mistakes before they get into print. For example, she recently received galleys from a career magazine and found they had spelled her name wrong in the byline. She called the editor right away and they fixed the blooper before it was published.

The moral of the story: It's always good to take a gander at your article before it goes to press. Not all publications will let you review the edited version of your article, but it never hurts to ask.

This is especially important if you've signed a contract where you guarantee everything contained in the article is true. What happens if one of your editors changes a fact or quote? Can you still guarantee that your article is free from error? Of course not. That's why, if you're forced to sign a contract with an indemnification clause, you should insist the contract also include a clause promising you a look at the article before it goes to the printers or online.

Let the magazine's fact checkers and proofreaders handle the factchecking because that's their job, not yours.

If you interviewed the Reverend Doctor Jerzy Sczyzlowski, Ph.D., M.D., R.D., why bother checking and rechecking that you got his name, title, and affiliations right? And if a source gives you a statistic, don't get your pants into a knot double-checking it. After all, that's why magazines have fact checkers—to check your facts. Right?

The fact checkers are indeed there to check your facts, so if you make a minor mistake, with their help it might not make its way into print or online. But they do work in the same building as the editors, and they do talk. If you commit too many faux pas, your editor will find out, and he'll think you did a sloppy job on the article. And you know what? He'll be right. "Writers should double-check their facts, stats, and quotes," says Jeremy White of *Pizza Today*. "That's part of being professional and accountable. If we turn up too many inconsistencies, that tells us the writer rushed through the process and is not worthy of another assignment."

"[Not fact checking] reflects poorly on a writer, such that we probably won't work with him or her again," says Kaja Perina, editor-in-chief of *Psychology Today*. "Writers should not leave fact checking to others for the simple reason that many magazines—this one included—cannot afford to fact check each piece." And that's another reason to do your own fact checking: Many magazines skip this step altogether, meaning any errors are on your head.

As good business practice, we always double-check our quotes, keep meticulous research notes, and provide our editors with the names, email addresses, and phone numbers for our sources. We don't have to be told. "You would never hand in a paper and expect your professor to fact check it—you'd fail," says Nancy LePatourel, former editor-in-chief of *Glow* magazine. "Why would you do anything less for your career?"

Besides, fact checkers make mistakes, too. Our names are going to be on these stories, and we're not willing to put our trust into a magazine fact checker or proofreader whose name won't be in 12-point type above the article.

BREAK THIS RULE

Never show an article to the source.

This is a biggie: Journalism teachers and other experts insist that showing an article to a source pre-publication is a breach of journalism ethics. But really, it depends on the type of article you're writing. And some publications, such as certain custom pubs, actually *require* you to do so!

Of course, you should never give sources a sneak peek at a controversial exposé, where they may want to fiddle with quotes and rebut statements from other sources in the article after the fact. But as-told-to articles and profiles? You can make a case for showing these to your sources. "I write a lot of as-told-tos, and a lot of health stuff," says freelance writer Leslie Pepper. "I frequently show articles to sources. For the as-told-tos, I want to make sure they're happy with the article. It's their story. For the health stuff—I want to make sure I'm right!"

The same goes for complicated scientific pieces or articles with a lot of jargon. "I always show passages to the source when writing about scientific subjects, which I do regularly," says freelance writer Dan Ferber. "It's saved me from a lot of errors. The risks are overblown: Just tell the source to check for accuracy, call the changes 'suggestions,' and veto them when necessary. What matters is whether the writer has control over the content and tone of the piece, not how he checks facts."

Linda would never show an article intended for a consumer publication to the source unless required by the editor, but when she was starting out she routinely showed completed trade magazine articles to her sources before turning the pieces in. She often wrote on complicated topics like reprographic printing processes and call center technology, and figured showing the articles to the sources was an easy way to check her facts. The sources were usually very good about pointing out factual errors, and her editors never expressed any concerns about this practice.

This practice did backfire on Linda once. She interviewed a UK-based company for an article about new printing technologies. For a week after she sent the article for a pre-publication review, she received desperate, early-morning calls from the company's PR person insisting Linda give the company more play in the article, change quotes to put the company in a better light, and attribute quotes given by other people to the company's source. By this time, Linda had developed more confidence in her writing abilities, and spurred on by this annoying person, she decided to save time by no longer giving sources sneak peeks at her articles. So be warned—if you regularly show your articles to sources, at some point you will assuredly get an overbearing company rep calling you at all hours.

In any case, always check with your editor before sharing a story; some have strict rules against the practice, while others prefer it. "I think it's a good idea," says Elisa Bosley, editor-in-chief emeritus of *Delicious Living*. "That way the source knows his or her words and thoughts are being represented accurately. [It] saves time for the fact checker." *Family Circle* at one point even required that writers double-check quotes with sources.

What if your source wants to see the article before you turn it in and this goes against your better judgment or your editor's rules? Tell him you're not allowed to show him the whole article, but you'll ask the editor whether it's okay to read his quotes back to him over the phone, or send him the quotes in an email.

You must format your article like a proper manuscript.

Newer writers especially get caught up in this "requirement," spending loads of time formatting their completed articles with one-inch margins, a double-spaced body, their name and address in the upper left corner of the first page, and their last name, article title, and page number in the upper left corner of all following pages. This is something that's often required with book manuscripts, and it made sense in the days when writers submitted hard copies of their articles. But for magazine articles these days, not to mention almost any other type of writing assignment, it's completely unnecessary.

Editors prefer to receive completed assignments digitally as an attached Microsoft Word file or within the body of an email message. Start off with the article title, your name, and the word count up top, the article below, and a list of your sources and their contact information at the end. No matter how you format the article—single spaced or double spaced, hard returns or indented paragraphs—if the editor wants it in a different way she can make it happen with the click of a button. The one thing editors don't like, however, are double spaces after a period instead of one space, a throwback to the days of typewriters. If you're hitting the spacebar twice after a period, train yourself to hit it only once and you'll stop dating yourself.

For blog posts and other content writing, editors will sometimes have you submit your copy right into their online platform, such as Wordpress, complete with formatting. One blogging client recently asked Linda to paste her post into a Google Doc, do the HTML formatting, and share it with the editor. In cases like these, of course, you don't need to follow standard manuscript formatting rules.

When it comes to things like how publications handle abbreviations, serial commas, titles, and so on, you *do* want to get these right. Sometimes, a publication will have its own style sheet, which is a document that tells the writer how to format and turn in articles. Ask your editor if she has one. She'll probably be impressed that you even know what a style sheet is. If they don't have one, you can do what Diana does and review articles in the publication that are similar in length and style to the one you're writing. Note how the magazine handles abbreviations, titles, and attributions, and follow their lead on your final copyedit of the article. Your editor will appreciate the extra effort, and anything you do that pleases an editor has a surprising tendency to translate into more dollars for you.

RENEGADE RULE-BREAKER

Damon Brown

Damon Brown cracked *Playboy* magazine, and went on to write books, develop apps, and much more.

Tell us about the article you sold to *Playboy*.

It's on emulation, a way to play old-school arcade games like Pac-Man and Donkey Kong on your computer. An emulator fools your PC into thinking it is a traditional video game machine you find in the arcade. Most emulators are free, designed by programmers who have a love of older video games. Unfortunately, the legality is questionable at best—Nintendo, Sega, and all these companies still own the copyrights to these games! So it's a hot-button issue. Video game historians are often advocates for emulators, as unlike book libraries or videotape archives, there are no official historical museums for classic arcade games. They just go away.

How did you break into *Playboy*?

Shortly after I started freelancing I went to an alumni get together and met Mary-Beth Bruno, then tech editor for Playboy.com. This was the winter of 2000. On the spot I pitched her a feature on the first lesbian video game, Fear Effect 2. She was responsive and asked me to send her my clips. We talked back and forth for a month and they seemed interested (even though my clips were light!), but then a controversy erupted over the ad campaign, which said of the female protagonists something like, "The only video game capable of 13 climaxes," referring to the multiple game endings possible—and, of course, alluding to something else. The story was assigned immediately after that. It ran March 2001. I found out later that they didn't really use freelancers! That's when I learned to always go for something, even if it seemed "impossible."

However, it took me four more years to get into *Playboy*, which is a whole different animal. Playboy.com was less responsive to my other queries, and the magazine wasn't responsive at all. In early 2003 I emailed and, later, cold-called the senior editor with a feature idea. He talked to me and asked me to send a query. We went back and forth for a month or two, but he ended up rejecting it in the end. About a year later the magazine ran a similar story. It bothered me, but it taught me that there is such thing as being too ahead of the curve.

Finally, in 2004 I attended the One-on-One, a small but intense conference in Chicago where you meet with up to four magazine editors for short, five-minute meetings. One of the editors was Chip Rowe, senior editor at the time for *Playboy*. He and I hit it off immediately. He liked all my ideas—I crammed about six in the five minutes—and though he wasn't the deciding editor on any of them, he gave his blessing for me to contact them and tell him that *he* sent me. It was an honor.

I went home excited, typed up the queries the next night, if not that evening, and sent them. Unfortunately, the other editors weren't as excited about my ideas. I didn't hear anything. I followed up a few times and still got no response. The conference was in July 2004 and, by the following year, I pretty much forgot about it. Then I woke up one random February morning—honestly—and my first thought was "You know what? I'm emailing *Playboy* new ideas now, dammit!" I did. The video game editor responded within a day to my two queries in that email. The first pitch they had just written about in the issue going to press. The second pitch was on emulators.

What challenges did you face in becoming a freelance writer, and how did you overcome them?

Many writers I know have to build up their ego to get out there. I have the opposite problem: If I believe in something enough, I'll run right onto the battlefield. That's exactly what happened when I decided to become a freelancer. I had little to no savings, and, since I was in school, my clips were old. My contacts from previous journalism gigs had dried up. In short, I had no network to pitch to and no clips to create that network. I think it's key to have at least five editors who you know will be responsive to your clips. I had none.

I did two things that helped me survive. One was that I cultivated mentors. Three of my former professors were freelancers when they were my age, so I'd have lunch with them—buy them lunch when I could!—and pick their brains. They loved it because they knew I was hungry. When you are dead set on doing something, on starving, fighting, working your ass off to make something happen, people can sense it. I think they respected that in me, so they helped guide my new career. I'll never forget that.

Second, I got a part-time job. A few of them. I could type 60 words per minute, knew AP style by heart, and worked at some pressure-cooker publications with equally intense editors, so I was well suited for jumping into a corporate environment for a week or two, handling my business, and going home to write. It was a tough grind for the nine months I worked as a full-time freelancer sending queries and as a temp, but it was well worth it. At my final temp job, as an assistant at the Academy of Nutrition and Dietetics, I would introduce myself as "Hi. I'm Damon. I'm a freelance writer, but I also work for the doctor down the hall."

People would sometimes laugh at my somewhat hubristic introduction, but most would ask me what I wrote about. I'd tell them. I said this to one woman in the copy room who responded "Are you? I'm Jennifer and I'm the editorial manager of the *Journal of the Academy of Nutrition and Dietetics*. Do you want to write about science?" I gave a loud "Yes!" That's how I got my first regular freelancing gig, and five years later, they're still one of my best clients.

Have you broken any "rules" in becoming successful as a freelance writer? If so, what were the rules, and how did you break them?

I signed a work for hire with Playboy.com, which I was taught by both journalism schools I went to that that was a no-no. However, that Playboy.com clip got me more places than any amount of resale money was worth. Sometimes you end up cutting your nose to spite the face. I try to avoid that.

I also believe in sharing insights. I learned this a while ago from a competitor in video game journalism. At the time there were only about four well-known video game journalists, and this guy was one of them. In short, I wanted his spot. I came up with a good video game pitch for a men's magazine and—lo and behold—he was the contributing editor of the section, so I'd have to pitch him. At first I was apprehensive about sending the idea, but I did. He not only loved the idea, he was supportive of me when the story started to go in another direction (especially helpful since I was doing the story from Japan!).

We remained writer colleagues, and have always tried to help each other out even though he's moved on to other publications and I've gotten more into books. More recently, a good freelance buddy of mine, Jeanette Hurt, and I will go back and forth about potential target markets, book ideas, and even writing rates. Sharing with others gives you clarity and objectivity, two things that are necessary to survive as a freelancer. You simply can't make it alone and the cliché is terribly true: You don't know where someone will end up.

What's the best piece of advice you've been given on writing (or the business of writing)? The worst?

Two pieces of advice, the first from Northwestern Professor David Standish, the second from a former agent of mine. It was in the beginning of my magazine freelancing career. I was starting to realize that I wasn't going to be able to make ends meet on freelancing alone. I took David to lunch and, totally stressed out, said that I thought I should take a corporate temp gig, but I wanted to stay true to writing. "I don't want to sell out," I said. He gave a warm laugh, shook his head and said "Damon, freelancing's always going to be there. You can leave and come back. No one does only freelance writing for 30 years or they get burnt out. Don't be afraid." And he was right. It was always there.

And from a former agent who, when swimming in a sea of rejections of a book we both *knew* was brilliant, said two things: "The path of brilliance is a lonely one" and, most importantly, "This is a marathon, not a sprint." I have the latter posted on my desk wall.

Do you have any advice for new writers who are looking to break in?

Write about what you love. I write about science, sex, technology, and music—four things I never get sick of! I just completed my first book, the *Pocket Idiot's Guide to the iPod* and you know what? I hate iPods now! If you're going to be dealing with tight deadlines, critical feedback, and sometimes underwhelming results, you're going to need to be passionate about it. If you can't get passionate about aluminum siding trade journals, you should keep the time you write for them limited.

Secondly, no matter how good of a writer you are, it will take time. Not only time for editors to know and trust you, but for you to get your writing to a higher professional level. Editors at *Playboy*, *SPIN*, and other publications are publishing me not only because my writing is stronger now, but also because I've been querying them for five years! They know my ideas, and some editors I've actually gotten a relationship with strictly through rejections. Remember it's a marathon. Think about building a career, not the next juicy clip. Because once you get into your dream publication, what's next?

It's been ten years since you spoke to us. How has your career changed?

A bit has changed! The breakthrough article for Playboy.com became the basis of my first major book, *Porn & Pong: How Grand Theft Auto, Tomb Raider and Other Sexy Games Changed Our Culture* (Feral House 2008). It put me on the road and I realized I absolutely loved public speaking. I had spent years researching these obscure topics and, suddenly, I had people excited to argue and discuss them. The speaking got me connected to the TED Conferences and, in 2014, I did my own TED Talk, "The Positive Power of Observation," on the conference's second stage. I also founded an app, called So Quotable, which allows you to capture cool things people say during a conversation, and that minor hit led me to two other people to found Cuddlr, an app that connects people for hugs. Again, my main niche is understanding how technology connects us in an intimate way. In that context, founding a platonic cuddling app makes perfect sense. It was great timing, too, as, in fall 2014, the world needed a wholesome diversion: Cuddlr immediately went to #1 on the Apple App Store and had a quarter million users. The success allowed us to be acquired less than a year later.

The unusual part was that the two-year rollercoaster ride from book author to successful entrepreneur happened while I was the primary caretaker of my first baby. How was I able to be a fully engaged father while still being a strong entrepreneur? After living in Silicon Valley for years, I realized the belief that you have to sacrifice everything to make your entrepreneurial mark is a myth. (How renegade!) The experience turned into my Inc. Magazine Online column, Sane Success, and that inspired my new best-selling book series, *The Bite-Sized Entrepreneur*. All self-published, *The Bite-Sized Entrepreneur: 21 Ways to Ignite Your Passion and Pursue Your Side Hustle* was an Amazon Top 10 Startup Book and the follow-up *The Productive Bite-Sized Entrepreneur: 24 Smart Secrets to Do More in Less Time* has been featured in *Time*, *Fast Company*, and other major publications.

I now consult potential entrepreneurs on their action plan as well as established startups and media companies on their communication and productivity. My teaching hub, Paylancing.com, is where fellow bite-sized entrepreneurs can share insights, read new strategies, and learn how to balance their priorities.

It all comes down to showing that going after your passion doesn't have to be an either/or proposition. As far as my journey, it has always been about showing how technology connects us; I just have changed the role from observer to narrator to creator. My palette is wider now.

Getting the Green: Don't Be Shy When It Comes Time To Collect

From hiring lawyers to pitching tents outside editors' offices, writers at times have to go to ridiculous lengths to get paid. When it comes to cutting checks, magazines sometimes seem to rank their writers—the people who supply the magazines' actual content—below every other contractor. Keep reading to find out how to break the rules that keep you from getting the money you've earned.

BREAK THIS RULE

Believe it when they say the check is in the mail.

We wince when we finally get an accounts payable person, editor, or publisher on the phone and he uses this cliché on us. In many cases, when we hear this line, we've already been told that the check is on someone's desk or in the bowels of the computer system or waiting to be signed by the senior vice president of human development, so by this point, we're fairly confident that no such check is in the mail.

We used to accept what our clients told us, thank them profusely, hang up, and spend the next fourteen days obsessively running back and forth to the mailbox, only to have a sheepish editor tell us our invoice didn't go through because they couldn't find our W-9s in their records.

Today we're a bit wiser. When an editor, an accounts payable rep, or the publisher tells Diana to hold tight because a check is in the mail, she holds off on her effusive thanks and instead asks for a check number and the date on the check so that her bookkeeper can watch out for it. (She may be her own bookkeeper, but she's very harsh with herself if the books aren't straight.) If they tell her the check has been cut but not mailed yet, she'll ask that they use FedEx to send it, especially if payment is seriously past due. And if they're within driving distance, she'll even say something like, "I'm so glad my check is ready. I can come over and pick it up now." Even if she's not in the neighborhood, chances are she has a trustworthy friend who's willing to pick up the check for her (see "BREAK THIS RULE: Don't use extreme tactics to get your money").

Beyond this, there's not a lot you can do besides keep following up until the check clears your account. The squeaky wheel and all that. Diana has actually turned down future work and backed out of assignments when she starts seeing a trend of late payments. Twenty years in the business has taught her that trend doesn't bode well for the publication's future.

BREAK THIS RULE

Don't bother the editor—she has nothing to do with you getting paid.

Writers who do things strictly by the books contact their clients' accounts payable department regarding all payment concerns. But the renegade way—going to your editor about late checks—can get you paid faster.

Diana once wrote for a business publication that was habitually slow in paying her. We're talking 60 to 90 days past due, with lots of annoying phone calls, pointed emails, and old fashioned begging and pleading with the accounts payable manager before she'd get her check. She'd always been told by other writers to go directly to accounts payable, but in this case, these people were oblivious to their obligation to pay for services rendered.

One day, Diana met her editor for lunch, an editor with whom she had an excellent working relationship. In fact, during the meal, her editor mentioned that she wished all of her freelancers were as headache-free as Diana. That's when Diana realized she had some leverage. When the editor asked Diana if she had any questions or concerns about the magazine, she responded, "As a matter of fact, I do. Is there anything you can do to help me get paid on time?" As the editor's face reddened with embarrassment, Diana explained that begging the company for her money was a huge headache and distraction.

The editor was appalled that her magazine was habitually late paying her. When they returned to the office, the editor brought Diana down to accounts payable, introduced her to the person who'd been ignoring Diana's phone calls and emails, and asked her to cut a check for all outstanding invoices ASAP. It was a sweet moment.

The way we see it, the accounts payable department is not interested in who you are or how dependable, professional, or fast you are. You're only a vendor ID number to them, another bill to be paid. Your editor, on the other hand, has much more at stake, especially if you have good history together. So why not use that relationship to your advantage? When your check is late, appeal to your editor first.

Remember to play nice. When Linda is checkless after 30 days (or whatever the contract's terms are), she emails the following note to the editor:

> *Subject line: Check the Check?*
>
> *Dear Susan:*
>
> *I was looking over my accounts and noticed that I haven't received a check for my article "Why I Love My Editor," which I turned in six weeks ago. Would you mind checking into this for me? Thanks!*
>
> *Cheers,*
>
> *Linda*

It's usually enough to start the payment wheels turning.

BREAK THIS RULE

Don't use extreme tactics to get paid, or you may not work for that magazine again.

There's an overarching "rule" in the freelance world that you should never, ever do anything to annoy your clients. They are the ones who hold all the power, after all.

However, if a publication is putting you off and you've exhausted every reasonable tactic to get a check, you may need to take extreme measures to get the payment you earned. Frankly, you shouldn't worry about angering clients who don't care about their writers. Do you even *want* to work for a publication that's dragging its heels to pay you? We know it sounds scary to burn bridges with a sub-par client, but believe us: There are plenty of publications out there that treat their writers well and pay them on time.

One of the best stories we've heard about a writer using extreme tactics to get paid involved a freelancer named Brett Forrest, who was owed almost $4,000 by *Gear*, which is—surprise, surprise—no longer publishing. He was sick of being told for months and months, "The check is in the mail," so he showed up at *Gear*'s offices with a tent, which he pitched in front of the publisher's office. After a few hours of camping activity and some back and forth between Forrest and the magazine's staff, *Gear* finally produced his money.

When Forrest was on his way out the door, his editor, who was in the last office before the exit, called him in. Forrest says, "He told me, 'Too bad we can't work together anymore. We could have worked something out.' Well, after 70 phone calls, I'm not sure that I could have done any more. He asked me not to tell anyone about what had happened, but I'd already told the *New York Observer*. As I was walking down the street, my cell phone rang and it was the editor. He said, 'I've got to hand it to you, that's what makes a good reporter.'"

Forrest admits he worried whether he was doing the right thing by using such an aggressive tactic to get his money, but he knew he didn't want to work for the magazine again. What's more, he says that the experience has made him more valuable to other editors he's worked with and who've heard the story. "They look at me and think, 'He's the kind of guy who can get me my story. He's not afraid.'"

Linda has never had to pitch a tent to collect a check, but she has used other extreme tactics to track down her money. When a Detroit-based newsstand magazine was more than eight months late paying Linda $1,300, she called and emailed daily, enlisted the help of a National Writers Union grievance officer, and reported the delinquent magazine to writers' organizations and publications. Still no check.

So Linda logged onto an online forum she frequents and offered $300 to anyone who would visit the magazine's office in person and demand the check. She immediately heard from a Detroit native named Lisa who was glad for the chance to make a buck and help out a fellow forum member. Lisa emailed the editor to tell him she was stopping by on X date at X time. When she got there, the receptionist had the money waiting for her. Unfortunately, the payment consisted of three checks, two of them post-dated, and one of which bounced—but Linda did get $800 of her payment in the bank before the magazine folded a few weeks later.

Here are a few other tactics to consider:

File a small claims suit.

We're surprised at the number of freelancers who have told us, "It's not worth going after the publisher." Many times, the threat of a small claims suit is enough to push a publisher to cut a check. Every state has its own small claims procedures; call your local small claims court for more information. Be aware, though, that your case may not be heard for months; three claims Diana filed in Massachusetts in October 2002 weren't brought before the court until April 2003. The sooner you file a claim for overdue funds, the less time the publisher has to split town.

Enlist the aid of the National Writers Union.

If you're a member of the NWU, you can look to their Grievance and Contract Division for help. Volunteer union members will contact the errant publication on your behalf and work out a payment agreement.

Hold your next article hostage.

If you're working on an assignment when a check is overdue, tell your editor, "I know this piece is due next week, but I can't afford to work on it until I'm paid for the other work I've done." You're putting your editor in a tough spot—he potentially has a gaping hole in an upcoming issue—but now you've made your headache his headache. Diana did this with a book publisher that hadn't sent the first of three payments yet, and the final portion of the book was due. When Diana said she wouldn't be sending in the final manuscript until she was paid, the publisher that wasn't able to take the time to pay Diana over the previous couple of months suddenly managed to FedEx her past-due check.

Report the delinquent publication.

Report the non-paying client to organizations like the American Society for Journalists and Authors (ASJA), the NWU, and writers' publications like Writers Weekly and Writer Beware. Writers' organizations usually alert their members to non-paying markets, and many writers' publications will post a warning to writers that they shouldn't accept work from the delinquent client.

Use social media.

We've never done this, but we wouldn't be above doing it, especially if we've exhausted all other avenues: Write about your efforts to get paid by a delinquent publisher on social media, especially if the magazine has a strong online presence. Writers typically protect their own, so we'll tend to spread the word quickly when a writer is being taken advantage of. Moreover, social media managers are tasked with keeping their employers' names in a good light, so your public complaints about late payments might be resolved much faster than if you were to continue calling and emailing the publication.

Even if you follow all these suggestions, you may never be paid, but by sharing information and complaining loudly, at least you can save other writers from the same sad fate.

BREAK THIS RULE

If you signed a contract,
you can't renegotiate payment for an assignment.

Your editor at *Sewage Monthly* assigned you 1,000 words on trends in sewage management. You've turned in the assignment on time, and she says the article looks great—but the following Thursday, she asks you to interview two other sewage experts, add their quotes to the article, and also provide her with two 200-word sidebars. Oh, and can you get this done by Monday morning? You check your contract, and it stipulates three interviews, which you did, and there's no mention of sidebars.

Many freelancers would simply grit their teeth and get to work, complaining about the unfairness of it all. They figure they signed a contract, so the editor has every right to ask for changes.

Changes are fine, and as much as we hate to break it to you, so is a complete rewrite. But should you roll over and play Kick Me Harder when an editor asks for more than what was contracted? No way. If an editor asks for work that's not included in your contract, that means you can—and should—ask for additional compensation.

A good contract will spell out what is expected of the writer. Many magazines will give writers the option of doing a rewrite (or two) before it foists a kill fee on them. One consumer magazine advised Diana ahead of time that they *always* asked for rewrites—their editorial department worked that way. But sometimes magazines offer unclear contracts, which spells bad news for newbie freelancers or writers who are uneasy with confrontation.

As part of their efforts to provide exceptional customer service, Diana and Linda often throw in a couple of sidebars with their stories without being asked—and they don't charge for them. Ninety-nine percent of the time, these sidebars take all of five minutes to create because they use leftover research and quotes from their interviews that didn't fit into the main copy.

But some magazine editors can't stop asking for more-more-more, even when you think you've gone above and beyond the written contract. You have a few options:

1. You can do the additional work with a smile.
2. You can ask for a kill fee.
3. You can call your editor and renegotiate the assignment.

We think the third option is the sanest. If you're feeling trod upon, figure out how much it will take for you to feel better and ask for it. This conversation doesn't have to be confrontational. Spell out the situation to your editor: "You've asked me to add two 200-word sidebars and include additional research in my article that will bring the word count well above the 1,000 words we agreed upon." Then, present a solution: "I estimate this is an additional 500 words above the assigned amount, plus time for more interviews and research, so I think you'll agree it's fair to amend the contract for the extra work."

If you're doing this in an email, no sweat. By phone? Present your solution matter-of-factly, with no tentative, permission-hungry, wishy-washy tone to your voice. If the editor rules out the extra payment, you'll need to decide whether she's a client you can't afford to lose, or a client you can't afford to keep. But either way, at least you've taken action rather than seethed in front of the computer all weekend.

If your article is killed,
be satisfied with the kill fee.

In many of the contracts that land on your desk, you'll notice a clause that goes something like this: "If the article is deemed unacceptable by the editor after the writer has been given the chance to remedy the situation, then a kill fee of X percent of the contracted amount will be paid to the writer." Kill fees usually run from 10 to 25 percent of the article fee; many freelancers negotiate up to 50 percent. Negotiating a higher kill fee is a lot like making a prenuptial agreement: You have every intention of things working out, but if they don't, you want to walk away with as much money in your pocket as you can.

No writer likes having her article killed, but sometimes taking a partial payment and being set free feels good, such as when you've done a couple of rewrites on your story and your editor still isn't satisfied. You may even broach the subject of the kill fee with her, especially if you know you'll have no trouble finding a new home for the story. Diana once wrote an article for a newly launched golfing magazine. She handed it in to her editor. That editor quit soon thereafter, and the article went off to another editor, who also quit. A third editor came along, who didn't bother to answer Diana's emails or telephone calls. Finally, when she heard this editor had also left, Diana knew this magazine was going nowhere fast and approached the editor-in-chief about getting her kill fee. Within weeks, the money was in her pocket—and a good thing, too, because the magazine shut down soon thereafter.

A good contract will spell out what kind of kill fee will be paid if the article is deemed unacceptable for publication. The writer can then walk away from the project with a bit of coinage in her pocket, free to sell the story to a more appreciative magazine. But kill fees lean toward the evil end of the moral scale when publishers and editors use them to satisfy their flaky whims. It stinks when you've done your work and your editor says she's satisfied with it, but you hear nothing until a month later, when the editor calls and announces chirpily, "We're killing the article because it doesn't fit with our new editor-in-chief's vision. Your kill fee is in the mail."

Try hiring a contractor to paint your home's interior walls in Williamsburg Blue and Colonial Red, and then telling him when he's finished, "I'm not going to pay you for this work because I changed my mind—I'm going in the direction of Concord Grape." He'll laugh as he holds out his hand for the money you owe him. And how would your editor feel if her publisher came up to her in the hallway and said, "Hey, Jane, great work editing those stories we'd planned for the next issue, but since we're going in another direction, we won't be paying your salary for that week"? This sums up how many publications treat their freelancers.

Linda went through this kill-or-be-killed experience in early 2005 when *Sly*, a magazine covering all that's wonderful about Sylvester Stallone, killed an article, claiming the mag had already scheduled a piece on the same topic. Linda's response? "Too bad—you assigned me this article, I gave you what you wanted, now you have to pay me. I'm not going to take a pay cut just because you goofed your own editorial schedule." Linda received a check for the full amount due her.

Should this happen to you, first check your contract for the wording, but then request your full fee, explaining that the kill fee covers work that is unsatisfactory, not untimely (at least from the magazine's new and improved perspective). Many editors will agree and go to bat to get you the full fee, or at the very least, a greater percentage of money than the kill fee specified. You won't know until you ask—and unfortunately, many freelancers sit back and wearily accept the kill fee instead of standing ground.

You have a lot of checks coming in, so go ahead and buy that new car/fancy watch/overseas vacation!

In good economies and bad, freelancers are usually the last in line to get paid. Magazines know that we writers have little clout compared to the printer or the magazine's staff, so they can (and do) string us along. One of Diana's old clients was supposed to pay 60 days after acceptance, but they regularly went to 90 or 120 days, despite a lot of badgering, pleading—and, finally, legal threats.

We're not trying to scare you; we only want to warn you, especially if you're new to the freelancing game, that checks seldom appear when they're supposed to, so don't go crazy on your credit line, figuring a whole wad of checks will appear like they're supposed to in your mailbox next week. The most successful freelancers have a lot of money in the pipeline, so something's usually coming in (even if it was due months ago), and they also sock some of their freelance windfall away for the lean times.

You don't need to send an invoice.

We've heard this from many an editor: "Don't worry about an invoice; we'll submit the paperwork for you." That's lovely and we thank them profusely for expediting payment, but we still invoice our editors to keep our *own* records in order.

Having a basic accounting system will help you tremendously at tax time. Moreover, if you have a lot of checks coming in or you're doing a lot of work, you can often forget who owes you and who has paid. A simple accounting system, updated weekly, will keep your business humming along nicely. It doesn't have to be fancy—a spreadsheet to track expenses and income suffices—and you can easily create an attractive invoice template in a word processing program. (Search for "free invoice template Word" and you'll find plenty of options.)

Diana successfully worked off a Microsoft Excel spreadsheet and Word invoicing system for a couple of years, but being the app junkie she is, she was lured by clever ad copy into using QuickBooks. While a wonderful accounting package, QuickBooks was overkill for her needs. So she had her husband help set up business accounts on Quicken, the software program she uses for her everyday finances.

Linda uses Freshbooks, a cloud-based accounting system for small businesses that costs $25 per month for up to 50 active clients (and $15 per month for up to 5 clients). Freshbooks lets Linda send invoices that can be paid via check, PayPal, or credit card; automatically logs payments; sends a weekly email summary of accounts receivable; and generates reports like profit and loss statements.

Even if your editors don't strictly require you to send an invoice, we suggest doing so anyway; it can help you track your income, and will also be useful should you need to go after a late payment.

RENEGADE RULE-BREAKER

Melanie Nicsinger

Melanie Nicsinger's very first clip came from *Parenting* magazine, proving that you *don't* have to start at the bottom.

When did you decide to become a freelance magazine writer, and why?

2005 is the first year I added magazine writing to my freelance business, but I've been a corporate writer for over 10 years—four of them freelance. I decided to try magazine writing because I was bored writing brochures and marketing materials. It was never the kind of writing I meant to be doing, so that year I made it a goal to get published and start building my clips.

How did you break into *Parenting* magazine? Was it your first national clip?

Parenting was my first clip, national or otherwise! I think what helped me break in was targeting the right editor. Also, since I was totally new, I tailored my approach in the same tone, language, etc. of the magazine hoping it would serve as a "sample" of my writing style.

What challenges have you faced as a writer?

The biggest challenge for me was letting go of the idea that I could only write corporate copy. By being willing to take a risk and step out of my comfort zone, I was able to get motivated by the challenge of trying something new instead of being intimidated by it. I pushed the pause button on that 'fear of failure' tape most writers play in their heads and accepted that an editor's rejection wasn't about me, personally, it's a business decision.

What's the best writing or business advice you've gotten?

Your book taught me to turn an "encouraging" rejection from an editor into a business connection. The that-idea-didn't-work, but-feel-free-to-send-more kind of response would have made me scurry away before I learned to take it literally and send more ideas! I've been shocked at how approachable most editors are. If they think the idea is good, they'll tell you. That's great motivation for a beginner, even if it doesn't result in a sale.

What's the worst writing or business advice you've gotten?

To start building your clips by writing for local, low-pay/no-pay markets. I was planning on taking this route until I read *The Renegade Writer*.

What "rules" have you broken so far in your career?

Wow, which ones haven't I broken! The two that stand out are, "Don't email editors" and "Start at the bottom." The first saved my queries from sitting around for weeks in a slush pile, and the second snagged me a national magazine for my first clip! Mostly, it's the entire renegade attitude of being bold, while at the same time being professional.

Do you have any advice for aspiring freelance writers?

If you're lean on clips like I was, make your queries "mini-clips." Use them as an opportunity to showcase your writing skills so the editor will know you can get the job done. Also, when you get any encouragement at all from an editor, run with it. Don't see it as a rejection, see it as being close to acceptance!

It's been ten years since you spoke to us. How has your writing career changed? What are you working on now?

Besides writing for *Parenting* again, I continued to write for corporations and also several regional business and lifestyle magazines. I landed a regular healthy lifestyle column in one of the regional magazines and it led me to deepen my life-long interest in natural health.

Over the last few years, I've shifted away from writing for magazines and corporate work into being a nutritionist and yoga teacher. I write all of my educational programs and online course content, and I think it helps me tremendously to have the business skills from being a freelance writer.

I'm still a renegade at heart. I never play small, I don't let rejection get in my way, and when I feel like I have a good idea, I run with it. This year I hosted my first women's yoga and wellness retreat to empower women, and it was a great success. I have a new passion thanks to the renegade attitude!

CHAPTER 8

The Renegade Attitude: Your Success Often Depends On Your Mindset

Successful freelancing is all about banishing bad attitude—the attitude that you're a supplicant instead of a professional service provider, that editors are against you, that writing gigs are few and far between, that leads and ideas are meant to be hoarded. You can easily develop a loser mindset when dealing with reticent sources, ridiculous rewrites, and non-paying magazines, but if you let this happen, you'll come to hate the writing life. Here are the bad-attitude rules you need to break today.

Keep editorial relations strictly business.

Contrary to what many writers tell you, editors are not overworked and underpaid liberal arts grads who resent us because they're frustrated writers themselves. We've found that magazine editors are generally an amiable lot who enjoy editorial work more than writing. Should you find yourself on the receiving end of lots of assignments from them, don't be surprised if you become friendly with one or two (or more!) editors, especially if you've visited them in person and you're no longer merely a faceless name who turns in great copy.

But before visions of schmoozy, table-hopping meetings in New York take over your fantasy life, let's take a reality check. Unless you're a Tom Junod, an Elizabeth Gilbert, or a hot, young British import, you probably won't be wined and dined next time you're in town, but you certainly can enjoy some perks that less valuable freelancers won't experience.

The reality is that although you may never break bread with the big guys, you can build a friendly relationship with the editors you work with continually. You start out with a lot in common—a love of language and a commitment to the magazine—so usually some kind of personal relationship develops once you start working together. Diana, for instance, has developed a variety of professional relationships with her editors. One editor, who's assigned her lots of shorts for two different magazines, has never met with her in person, but their emails and telephone calls are friendly, if not chatty. Another editor both Diana and Linda know went freelance, and now they occasionally meet up to talk shop.

It's hard to work with an editor on assignment after assignment and not build a rapport—and why should you prevent a genuine friendship from developing in the name of acting "professional"? Diana strives to keep communications with her editors friendly, yet businesslike, by imagining they're co-workers sitting on the other side of the building. She wouldn't send co-workers stiff, formal missives, and she also wouldn't forward chain-mail virus warnings or text them yesterday's memes.

Linda sends her editors Christmas cards, plus small gifts when they get married, have a baby, or land a new job or promotion. After all, these are the people who keep her mortgage paid...why not treat them nicely?

Linda's husband Eric lets editors see his funny side. In a list of ideas he sent to his editor at *Woman's Day*, he included, "15 Ways to Achieve Nuclear Détente in Your Neighborhood." Did his editor snap back with a disgusted email? Did she vow to never work with this unprofessional writer again? No—she laughed and assigned him another idea off the list. Lastly, Diana, who profoundly misses *Spy Magazine*, created a cheeky and slightly naughty version of an article she'd written for an online magazine and sent it to another editor at the same magazine. He liked it so much, he included it on a satirical website he set up with his editor friends.

You don't necessarily have to send gag emails to your editors to make them love you. Sometimes it's fine to let your hair down, so to speak. Writer Bethanne Kelly Patrick landed a contributing editorship with a newsstand magazine simply by heading off to a comedy club with a bunch of writers and editors. "The editor of the magazine and I hit it off," she says. "Thank goodness he likes my work, too!"

As a professional or aspiring freelance writer, you know not to scrawl your pitch letters in crayon on cocktail napkins, and you know enough to hand in articles that are on time and on target. But don't let your professional demeanor get in the way of establishing friendly relationships with your editors.

BREAK THIS RULE

Editors pay your rent, so you should do everything you can to please them.

Most editors you'll meet during your career are pleasant, if not wonderful, people, but we'd be remiss in our duties if we failed to talk about the editors from the nether-regions of hell.

Some forget to forward our invoices to the accounting department, or they take forever to respond to our pitches. Others will ask you to write about one thing, then come back and tell you that they need it written *this* way. You turn that in, but, Oh no! It needs a second rewrite, but this time with a little of, oh, I don't know what! (But you are expected to know because you're a mind reader as well as a freelancer.) A few more rewrites, and then silence before you get the kill fee, which usually arrives way after your rent was due.

If you do run into an editor who's impossible to please, before refusing work from her, you may want to ask what you can do to make her happy. You can say something like, "The last article I wrote for you required so many revisions out of the scope of the original assignment that I had to turn down other work to make the changes. Is there anything we can do to make sure this doesn't happen again?" You can offer to turn in an outline for the editor to approve or suggest she give you more detailed article descriptions in the future. This demonstrates to the editor that you're willing to put forth the effort to make the relationship work. She may give you some good advice and—nice surprise—she may even come to the realization that her way of working is damaging her relationship with her writers.

However, while you should always be professional and do your best work, and give your clients the benefit of the doubt, it makes no sense to let yourself serve as a client's personal doormat. Sometimes, you need to drop a client and move on. Don't burn bridges by handing the editor a pink slip filled with profanities and accusations; instead, when she contacts you with another assignment, either decline the offer with no explanation or answer more directly that it's best for you focus on other work and wish her well.

Another option is to raise your rates to a level where you'll feel it's worth your time and energy to deal with this client. Diana did this with a local client who gave her a lot of migraines. One day she was in a meeting with the big boss, who informed her there were two types of writers—there was a top-tier and then there were "others, like you." Ouch! Even this guy's staff members winced. But upon reflection, Diana figured out that top-tier writers commanded more money, especially when they had to deal with a difficult client like him. The next time he asked her to quote on a project, she informed him she'd raised her hourly rate to $85. And you know what? He paid it.

Though Diana used this tactic with a copywriting client, it can also work for troublesome magazines and content clients. Money isn't everything, but sometimes it makes a painful job more bearable.

Freelance writing is an ultra-competitive field.

Linda asked several of her editors what percentage of the writers they hire turn in good work on time. The answer: Ten percent. Similarly, former *Shape* EIC Anne Russell says only ten percent of the pitches that cross her desk warrant serious consideration. She'll pass these pitches on to the appropriate editors, but out of those ten percent, she guesses that one percent result in an actual assignment.

The fact that 90 percent of the writers out there pose no competition for you is great news. Unfortunately, the writers who make up that portion of the freelancing population are constantly banging on your editors' doors, making it difficult for even the best writer's voice to rise above the din. And many of these sub-par writers have impressive clips that are more the result of their editors' hard work than of their own talents, which helps them lodge a foot in the door while you're still waiting outside. Only after trying—and being unsatisfied with—all those other writers will the editor be ready to give you a try.

Fighting your way through hordes of feeble freelancers is annoying, but take solace in the fact that if you're part of the 10 percent of writers that editors can depend on, once you finally wedge your foot in the door you'll never go without work. Keep marketing, turn in your very best work, and don't be discouraged by the "competition."

"Freelance Writer" is a euphemism for "unemployed."

If by "unemployed" they mean someone who doesn't work at a 40-hour-per-week salaried job with benefits, a daily commute, and an annoying co-worker in the cubicle next door, then we can see where it would appear that freelancers are "unemployed." It's an incorrect assumption, but understandable.

More often than not, though, when we hear this we know they're suggesting that a freelance writer is *unemployable*: they're assuming we're freelance because we've lost a "real" job and can't find work, or that we need to stick a job title after our names so it looks like we're not sitting at home all day eating Cheetos and watching *Project Runway* marathons on Lifetime. We've actually had people tell us to our faces that freelance equals unemployed. It used to make us mad and want to punch them in the nose (at least Diana wanted to punch; Linda is far less pugilistic). Now? We don't care what obviously mean and/or ignorant people think, so we shrug and find someone more interesting to talk to.

We started hearing the whole "freelance equals unemployed" blather when the publishing industry went into meltdown in the early '10s, and yes, a lot of editors who'd previously held staff jobs began freelancing. Whether they were serious about it or not, we don't really know, nor do we care. Concurrently freelancing has become more prevalent in many industries beyond publishing, so it's not such a big deal any longer to be a one-woman (or -man) enterprise. Still, we occasionally hear it from strangers, and occasionally from older family members who encourage us to get "real jobs" so we'll have pensions when we retire. Um, yeah.

If you can't let snide comments about your career roll off your back, you can try some gentle education. You could tell a concerned grandmother that you know writers who earn more freelancing than they did as attorneys at major law firms and that there are plenty of ways for free-lancers to save for retirement these days. Or if you're good with a witty comeback, nail the jerk at your spouse's holiday party with something like, "I do have to work harder to surpass what I made as a marketing manager at X Company, but it's wonderful not having co-workers. Would you excuse me please?"

BREAK THIS RULE

Eat cookies, punch a few pillows, and mope when you get a rejection.

As professional freelancers, we think writers should stop placing so much emphasis on rejections. If your work is rejected by an editor, it's a simple business decision: Your offer was not right for the publication at this time.

Rejection isn't about you. When you're approached by a salesperson at the supermarket asking if you want to sample a new brand of crackers and you say "No thanks," does that mean the salesperson is a terrible human being? Is it a judgment call on the actual person handing out the crackers? Or even on the quality of the product? No. Your rejection of the offer means you're full from lunch, or you can't eat gluten, or you're not in the mood for a snack, or you're a vegan and the crackers have cheese powder on them. The product doesn't stink, and neither does the salesperson. It has nothing to do with either of them.

It's the same with writing. They're not rejections—they're business decisions. What if your attorney or hairdresser moped around in their bathrobes like some writers do for days whenever they lost a potential client? Sure, your attorney or hairdresser might be disappointed, but if they are interested in staying in business, they'll focus on another case or book that open spot with a new client.

One of the gifts Diana received during her ten years working in advertising and marketing was a thick skin. Not only were her great ideas shot down with regularity, but they were shot down in public, with everyone watching—and sometimes laughing! What hurt more was when they were ignored. But one day she realized that her co-workers and clients weren't laughing at or ignoring *her*—they were laughing at or ignoring *her ideas*. It was nothing she needed to take personally. So when an editor shoots off a note to her saying, "This idea doesn't work for us," it's not half as bad as having copy ridiculed by an unhappy client.

BREAK THIS RULE

Writers are always being "taken" by the publishing industry.

You hear this woe-is-me mindset from freelancers on every online writers' forum: "Editors are out to get me! Every client wants something for nothing!"

However, while you may think editors' jobs consist of taking advantage of poor underpaid writers while they work jobs that are so much easier and more carefree, the opposite is more likely.

Here's one example: A few years ago, the editor of a restaurant industry trade magazine Linda knows hired a writer to profile a restaurant in California based on the writer's excellent query. The writer dragged his heels on the assignment, but finally turned in a piece that was so good that the editor decided to expand it into a feature.

When the editor tried to contact the owner of the restaurant to verify his quotes, the restaurant couldn't be located. The editor checked the restaurant guide and searched around online. Nada.

The editor then tried to contact the several suppliers who were quoted in the article, only to find out they didn't exist either. The writer had clearly made up the entire article. If the editor hadn't been diligent in his fact checking, this fakery would have run in the magazine, embarrassing the editor and the entire magazine staff. When the editor wrote to the writer to find out what the heck was going on, he received no response. (We assume the writer received no check in return, so there's that.)

Similar cases of writers turning fiction into fact include *The Boston Globe* columnist Mike Barnacle, who resigned in 1998 amid accusations that he fabricated the characters in a 1995 column, and Stephen Glass, a former staff writer for *The New Republic* who put one over not only on his employer, but also *Rolling Stone*, *George*, and other magazines with articles that included imaginary sources and fabricated quotes.

Imagine how many writers are giving editors the runaround in their quest to make a buck. Imagine trying to do your job with the stress of knowing that your writers could be scamming you. Then imagine dealing with prima donna writers who flip out over minor edits, writers who disappear at deadline time, and writers who turn in work filled with misspellings, grammatical gaffes, and factual fallacies. We know a lot of editors, and *whoa*, the stories they tell make us proud and grateful we're the writers they can depend upon for professionalism. Did we mention that on top of all this, editors have to work in an office with other people—gossipy co-workers and megalomaniac bosses? And you think doing revisions from the comfort of your home office is bad!

If you think you're the only one in the writer/editor relationship who's at risk of being taken advantage of, stop thinking like a victim and take charge of your business and attitude. Focus instead on making your deadlines, delivering copy that delights your clients, and being a pleasure to work with, and you'll find you're respected more than victimized.

BREAK THIS RULE

Leads are gold; don't share them with other writers.

Diana and Linda met on the internet. At first, they'd talk about projects they were working on. Then, Diana started writing for a magazine Linda wrote for regularly, which gave them more common ground. Soon they were sharing impressions about certain editors, information about who was changing jobs, or advice on what kind of stories Magazine X was looking for. More time passed, and they started giving each other leads or asking if they could use each other's names when approaching new editors.

Around the same time, Linda met another writer—we'll call him Chris—who wanted to pitch one of the magazines Linda was writing for. Linda gave him insight into the editorial needs of this magazine, and through her editor, Linda heard that Chris had used her name in his introduction letter, which Linda hadn't given him permission to use. Annoying, to say the least. To make things worse, the writer bollixed up the assignment, which didn't make Linda look too good in the eyes of her editor.

Over the next few months, Chris continued to ask Linda for help, and Linda, being the nice person she is, gave it to him. In fact, when Linda developed a closed mailing list for several writer friends for the purpose of sharing leads, she included this person in the group. While everyone else freely shared leads or magazine information, Chris contributed nothing.

Flash forward to the economy bottoming out. Linda, like many other writers, was finding it hard to place stories, but she heard through the grapevine that Chris had more work than he knew how to handle. So Linda wrote to him and said, "Hey, how about sharing a few names?" Response: silence. Linda never heard from Chris again.

Don't feel sorry for Linda; feel sorry for the tight-fisted writer. Chris learned only to take, not give—not a good strategy for a writer who wants to move ahead with his career. A few other writers on Linda's list noticed the same stingy qualities in this writer, so the group quietly disbanded, only to join forces again without him.

Diana and Linda now have several writer friends who share leads regularly, and they've broken into several magazines using advice from these friends. On the other hand, when Chris hits a slow time—and believe us, he will—who will he turn to for help?

Think other writers are your competition? Over the years, Linda estimates she's received well over $40,000 in work directly from fellow writers. They've passed her name along to their editors when they thought she would be perfect for an assignment they couldn't take on, and one writer even introduced Linda to an agent who ended up hiring Linda to write two Idiot's Guides at over $10,000 apiece.

Remember, some of your best resources in your freelance writing career are other writers; we tend to look out for one another, and want to see all writers succeed. Also keep in mind that there is plenty of work out there for us all. Holding on to a scarcity mindset when it comes to sharing leads with other writers will only result in less work for you in the long run. Be generous with information, and other writers will do the same for you.

Editors will steal your ideas.

In the twenty years we've been freelancing, we have sent hundreds of ideas to magazines, and in only a few cases do we think an editor stole our ideas. In one case, Linda sent a pitch to a regional magazine about a Boston man who had an interesting hobby. The editors sent Linda a rejection, saying they had already assigned that idea to a writer in-house, who had already interviewed her source. But when Linda spoke with the source for another article, he confirmed that he had not been interviewed by the magazine in question—in fact, they hadn't even contacted him yet. Pretty fishy.

In another case, Diana sent a pitch to a women's magazine, where the editor spent months asking questions about the profile subject before she could make the decision to assign. One day the profile subject called Diana, confused that another writer, whom she had never talked to before, had called her to schedule an interview for this article. When Diana called the editor and left a message, the editor emailed back with an apology, saying another writer had been assigned the profile awhile ago, which Diana knew to be a bald-faced lie as she had worked for months to gain the subject's trust in sharing her story. She resolved never to pitch this editor again, and she has warned other writers to stay away from her, too.

But such duplicity is extremely rare. Often, you'll suggest an idea to a magazine, get a rejection, and then, months later, see your very idea in that same magazine. You might suspect the editors stole your idea, but more likely than not they already had that idea in production when you queried them. With a million freelance writers fighting for page space, duplicate pitches happen often. Former *Shape* editor-in-chief Anne Russell says she would see five or six pitches a week on yoga. "None are unique, but the writers think they are," she says. "It's stunning how many writers will come up with the same idea at the same time."

Writers spend far too much time worrying about idea theft, and this leads them to write skimpy pitches to avoid sharing information that would allow the editor to run with the idea. This tactic only hurts the writer, as editors can't assign an article if they don't know exactly what it is.

Yes, clients do occasionally steal ideas. Other times, the fates play out so that it looks that way. As Russell says, "Magazines usually have a fairly limited subject area, a narrow focus, so editors have seen every idea under the sun." Why spend so much time worrying about it? If you feel someone has played fast and loose with your truly original idea, you can certainly call them on it, but if you want to keep earning, scratch the client off your list and keep on pitching elsewhere.

BREAK THIS RULE

Take every assignment an editor throws your way.

You'll hear many experts telling writers they should say yes to any assignment they can get, because to turn down work would insult an editor and you'll never get another chance. A 1,000-word assignment that pays $10? Don't you dare say no. An assignment from an editor who doesn't seem to know what he wants? Hey, it's money!

That may be okay advice for when you're starting out and desperate for clips and checks, or if you're super-eager to crack a certain publication. But after awhile, you have to learn to say no. Sometimes you're busy, the pay is less than what you need to earn to stay in business, or you're sick of jumping through hoops for a certain editor—so to keep your sanity or pay your bills, you have to say no.

For example, Linda once wrote for a business magazine that let every editor in the department edit her work. Whenever her articles came back for revisions, they were so covered with red ink it looked like the editors had sacrificed a goat on them. And many of the remarks were simply ridiculous. When Linda wrote that the color and movement of video displays help attract trade show visitors to your booth, one of the editors commented, "If color and movement attract visitors, why not just have a flashing blue light in your booth?" Yes, this editor seriously expected Linda to address in her 1,000-word article on trade show success why video displays are more effective than a flashing light. Linda gritted her teeth and patiently explained that there's a reason millions of Americans sit fixated in front of their TVs for hours each day and not in front of a flashing blue light.

Eventually, Linda refused to take any more assignments from this magazine. Due to all the time she spent on ludicrous revisions, her per-hour rate fell dangerously close to burger-flipping wages. Once she ditched this magazine, she had time to work on getting better assignments from better magazines—and get them she did.

In fact, if you don't learn to turn down assignments you'll never move up in the writing world, because you'll be too busy writing for all the 10-cent-per-word markets to have the time to pitch higher-paying ones. When Linda decided after a couple of years that it was time to raise her rates, she (nicely) told the editors at the low-paying trade magazines she wrote for that she couldn't work with them anymore, but her husband Eric, who was starting out as a freelance writer, would be happy to take on their assignments. This gave Eric a leg up in the freelancing world while giving Linda time to break into better markets.

RENEGADE RULE-BREAKER

Monica Bhide

Washington, DC-based food writer Monica Bhide has amassed an impressive number of clips during her freelance career.

You have cracked some very prestigious markets—the *Washington Post*, *The New York Times*, and *Food & Wine*, for example—that many writers find hard to break into. What has made the difference for you?

First, thanks for your very kind words. I guess to a certain extent in my case ignorance is bliss. I did not know, and in many cases still don't know, a lot about "cracking markets." I had no idea what a pitch letter was or how to approach an editor. I simply had some ideas on things I wanted to write about and either emailed or called the editors directly. I had no idea about rejections or how to "study the markets." In most cases I knew my subject and I knew what I wanted to focus on. They asked a ton of questions because I was so new and in one case even asked for a reference, which I happily provided. When the *NYT* story ran as the lead for the food section, I think I almost had a heart attack. Truly, it was not until they ran it and I started to learn about freelancing as a career that I realized how lucky I had been.

One of the main reasons I fell in love with your book was that it did not typecast writers or force freelancers into doing things a "certain way." Your book gave me exactly what I needed to write as I wanted to. I had no idea about sending clips, snail mailing letters or anything else. And your book said, "It's okay to do it your way" in essence. I think there is no right or wrong way to freelance. There is a different path and a different solution for each person in this career.

Why did you start freelancing?

Well, due to many personal circumstances and my desire to write, I quit my paying day job to become a writer. It was four months into the "new career" when someone asked me what I do. I said, "I am a writer" and she said, "You poor thing, do you freelance?"

What do you enjoy most about freelancing/writing? The least?

I love being able to write about what I want and when I want. There is so much out there that fascinates me and amazes me. I love it. The least? I guess it would have to be being typecast as "one type" of writer. I want to write about many different things.

What have you learned about writing/freelancing that has made a big difference to your work?

I have learned that the only thing that separates successful writers from others is persistence. Notice I don't say talent. That is a given. You have to keep trying and keep going. Believe me, that is easier said than done. But that is the difference that will make the difference.

It's been ten years since you spoke to us. How has your career changed?

What has changed—well, a lot and not much at the same time! I am, officially, an author. I have written seven books, including *Modern Spice: Inspired Indian Flavors for the Modern Kitchen* (Simon & Schuster), and more recently formed my own small independent press and just released my first food fiction title, *Karma and the Art of Butter Chicken*, which is getting wonderful reviews with readers! What hasn't changed: my view of what it takes to succeed in this business—persistence. I really see no other trait as being the most important trait any writer needs to succeed. Currently, I am working on my next novel—a fantasy novel—based in Washington, DC.

CHAPTER 9

Thriving Beyond Surviving: Reach For The Top

Maybe you've already landed assignments, but you can't crack the better-paying markets. Or maybe you're sick of the feast-or-famine lifestyle of the typical writer. It could be that you're limiting your prospects, not doing the right type of research, or missing out on marketing opportunities. Here, we debunk the common myths that keep you from getting what you want—and what you deserve—from your writing.

BREAK THIS RULE

You don't need a website.

True, having a website isn't *imperative*; many writers don't have one, and they do fine. But chew on this—Linda has gotten several assignments from editors who have run across her website, including a bi-weekly gig that lasted well over a year and netted her $1,400 per month.

When we wrote the first two editions of this book, you had two choices for website development: hire a web designer or spend hours building a site yourself. Today, you can get a professional-looking website set up in minutes with a few keystrokes and a valid credit card through companies like Weebly, Wix, Squarespace, and more—no advanced degree in computer programming required. If you're a true technophobe, ask anyone under the age of 30 to help you set this up. They'll be able to do it for you while simultaneously texting their friends and uploading videos to YouTube.

Even if you want a website that's totally original, you don't have to spend thousands of dollars on it. You have something web designers need—professional writing—and sometimes you can negotiate a barter with them. Years ago Linda traded her writing services for a professionally designed site, and then traded services with a different web designer when she wanted to redesign the site and add special coding. Her site drew tons of compliments from clients, and the only cost was her time!

Of course, if you like design and technology, the web is your oyster, so to speak. Diana created her first, very basic site with Dreamweaver and a rudimentary knowledge of HTML. Dozens of software programs out there will let you create a good-looking site, even if your design skills would give your elementary school art teacher the vapors.

Remember, editors aren't going to your site to be wowed by your JavaScripting or animated GIFs; they're there to see your words. Think of your website as your virtual business card; you wouldn't hand an editor a card covered with quills and scrolls and pictures of your six cats—so focus on getting your copy right and making your site easy to navigate, and forget all the digital gewgaws.

Here's what to include on your website to attract—and wow—clients:

A tagline that will help clients find you.

Carol Tice of Make a Living Writing suggests coming up with a tagline that reflects what clients will be looking for, but that won't put you in competition with thousands of other writers' sites. For example, if you choose "Freelance Writer" as your tagline, there's virtually no chance you'll come up even close to the first page of search results for that term because there are so many other "Freelance Writers" out there vying for work. However, "Raleigh Health Writer" can cut through the competition and help you attract the right clients.

A list of published work.

Linda divided her list into several categories, including health, women's, men's, business, and science/technology. Each article listing included the article title, the name of the magazine, the article's publication date, and a snappy bit that described the article topic (usually lifted straight from the article's lead paragraph).

Information on reprints.

Linda marked her articles with a red asterisk as they become available for reprint; if you earn a lot of money by reselling articles and are careful to sell only first rights, this could be a good option for you, too.

Clips.

You can link to your work that appears in online venues, and upload PDFs of print clips. Just be sure to grab copies of your online articles or posts with all the formatting, because sometimes links die...and you don't want your nice clips to die with them. Consider making PDFs or taking screenshots of your online clips.

Testimonials.

Linda asked for testimonials from her editors and then included them on her site. This "social proof" assures clients you can do the work.

A photo.

Diana included a picture of herself, so editors have a face to attach to her name. One big tip from Carol Tice of the Make a Living Writing blog is to be sure, if your headshot was taken at an angle, that you're facing towards your website copy, not off the edge of the screen.

A Hire Me page.

Many writers forget that the purpose of their site is to get writing clients to hire them. Use this page to push the benefits of working with you, recap what kinds of writing you offer, and give potential clients a way to get in touch.

If you decide to create your own site, check out other writers' sites and note what you like and don't like about them. You don't have to reinvent the web to achieve the same results on your site.

If you don't yet have a web site and this book inspires you to make it happen, be sure to purchase your own domain name instead of using an address like imthebestwriter.wordpress.com; it looks a lot more professional. You'll have to be creative to come up with a name that's not already taken, but don't fall into the trap of being too cutesy. Your name—www.jerzysczyzlowski.com—is always a safe bet.

BREAK THIS RULE

Once you have a full writing schedule, you'll know you've made it.

The temptation to sit back and enjoy the ride will be great, but don't be fooled: No freelance writer, no matter how good she is, can afford to sit back and cool her heels. Nothing lasts forever, including dream editors, lucrative gigs, bull markets, and plum assignments.

Over the course of two years, Linda lost four regular gigs. These losses of regular income (from $250 to $1,400 per month *each*) could have been deadly if Linda hadn't kept the marketing machine humming. Diana experienced such a slowdown after her maternity leave. When she returned to writing part-time when her son was a toddler, she felt like she was starting from scratch because the market had changed so much.

Unfortunately, when you take a break from marketing, whether it's to procreate your species or to take a six-month trip across Africa, be forewarned that when you return to your computer, you'll need to hustle to get back to where you were before you left. Magazines go belly-up and editors change jobs, so never stop researching new markets. And, ironically, when you're at your busiest is when you need to market yourself the most—otherwise, once you've busted your butt over your current batch of assignments, you'll find yourself with no work at all.

Keep those pitches circulating; since it can take months to land an assignment, the time to send pitches is *now*. The interviews and research you're doing should be good fodder for more article ideas, so spin off ideas and pitches from your current work. Even when you're super busy, try to set aside a few hours one day a week to reach out to editors. In a couple of months, when all your writing buddies are fretting about their lack of assignments, you'll be glad you put in the effort.

BREAK THIS RULE

Writing is the most important thing you do.

Correction: *Marketing* is the most important thing you do, at least when it comes to keeping your writing business afloat. Plenty of talented writers have no work because they don't know how to market themselves. Conversely, tons of sub-par writers get published because they know how to keep their names in front of editors. Remember the editors who told Linda that only 10 percent of published writers actually turn in articles on target and on time? The other 90 percent are mostly mediocre writers with good marketing skills. So imagine what a great writing talent like you could do with the right marketing! Here are some easy and fun ideas for marketing yourself beyond the basic pitch:

Keep yourself on your editor's radar.

Every few months, write to all the editors you've worked with to update them on your writing progress and let them know you'll soon be available for assignments. Linda usually writes:

> *Dear Editor:*
>
> *I hope all's well with you! Things have been going well here—I've recently completed articles for* Woman's Day, Men's Fitness, *and* Oxygen.
>
> *I'm starting to set my assignment schedule for November. Is there anything I can do for you at* Hireme Monthly *magazine?*
>
> *Thanks, and I look forward to your reply!*
>
> *Best regards,*
>
> *Linda Formichelli*

No matter how desperate for work you might actually be, never tell your editors that once your busy period ends, you have nothing on your plate. You want to come across as a successful, in-demand writer, so put a *positive* spin on your letter.

Take a road trip.

Linda and Diana trek to New York City to meet with editors for coffee, shoot the bull, and throw around article ideas. They also visit their local editors when they have the chance; for example, Linda's had a couple of coffee meetings with a Chapel Hill-based trade editor. Even if you're busy now, you can make plans to visit editors when the work lets up; set dates, create a travel itinerary, and come up with ideas you can pitch. Even if you get only one assignment from the trip, that one check will probably more than cover your travel expenses, which are tax deductible in any case.

Surf the web.

Keep on top of the news in the magazine industry by frequenting such websites as Media Life, Folio, and the American Society of Magazine Editors. When a new magazine is announced or an editor changes jobs, you can be one of the first to send an introductory letter or pitch. The same goes for other types of writing, like blogging and content writing: Stay up to date in your field by frequenting industry forums and news sites.

There are also fee-paying sites that will keep you updated on publishing news. Diana subscribed to Freelance Success for many years; the $99 annual fee deterred wannabes, so the members-only bulletin board wasn't cluttered with questions like, "What's a query letter?" or "Could someone here give me their editors' names?" Linda used to be the Other Den Mother at the Freelance Writers Den, which boasts a busy forum where writers can discuss the industry. By connecting with other writers, you'll hear about editors who are leaving or get wind of magazines that are in trouble long before the media find out.

BREAK THIS RULE

Feeling down? Ask your friends and family for encouragement and kudos.

Diana used to believe that one of the big perks of the writing life is fantasizing about how the mean girls in junior high gnash their middle-aged molars when they see her byline on newsstands. (Diana has matured in the years since the first edition of this book was released, and doesn't give a hoot what most people think of her anymore.)

The truth is, Diana's own mom doesn't read her articles, never mind those snarky girls from the Dark Ages of adolescence. That's why she's admitting this here; her mother *still* hasn't read this book, even after Diana mentioned she divulged some embarrassing family secrets in it.

In fact, only one of Diana's friends shows any deep interest in what she has written, and the rest are politely curious, totally oblivious, or, sadly, mildly jealous. This used to bug Diana, but then she put herself in her friends' shoes. When was the last time she jumped up and down over her college friend's latest successful PR campaign or another friend's much-lauded study of the economic impact of the oil and gas crisis in California? As freelancer Brett Forrest says, "You wouldn't go up to your uncle who works in a factory and say, 'Nice riveting.' As a writer, it would be nice to get that kind of attention, but I don't think it's realistic."

This was a tough lesson for both Linda and Diana. The people you think will be most happy for you may be the most indifferent or oblivious to your successes. Why? Who knows—but we're guessing that if they are truly good friends, they're happy for you, as you're happy for them when they get promoted or land a new job. They're just not going ask you in a humble tone of voice if they can kiss your ring.

On the flip side, your success may indeed stir up envy in friends and family members. After all, when they get a promotion or a new job, it's not as visible as a spread in *The Atlantic*. And how many of your friends and family members honestly love their jobs? Unfortunately, very few people are happy with the work they get paid to do. Even the best of friends can be driven to jealousy when they see someone close to them not only following their dreams but succeeding wildly with them.

So should you tuck your achievements under your hat or wear them proudly on your sleeve? We say do a little of both. We're careful not to gush too effusively about our latest accomplishments to friends and family members who generally withhold their encouragement. Instead, we save it for those who will get a kick out of our successes. (And if you hang out with people who make you feel really bad about your happiness, then we urge you to find new friends.)

BREAK THIS RULE

Most writers have drinking problems.

Ernest Hemingway. Dorothy Parker. Truman Capote. Hunter Thompson. Pete Hamill. The list goes on of journalists/writers who've used alcohol to make their words flow and sparkle. The image of the hard-drinking, ciga-rette-smoking journalist is a caricature in pop culture, and if you look at the writing profession as a whole and focus on the writers at the top of the heap, it seems like an awfully high percentage of novelists, as well as nonfiction writers, have needed alcohol to tap into their genius.

Diana's gotten a lot of "you're-a-writer-so-you-must-drink-like-a-fish-haa-haa" comments over the years, and they've always made her feel very uncomfortable. First, they imply she drinks heavily because that's what *all* writers do, and second, because she *does* have a family history of al-coholism, when she has the occasional drink, she's led to think, "Am I having this because that story due tomorrow is giving me fits? Is this the drink that will lead me down the road to rehab?"

The longer you walk the earth, the better you'll understand that alco-holism doesn't play favorites. Yes, a lot of writers have alcohol problems, but so do many professors, nurses, stay-at-home parents, politicians, teen-agers, and grandparents. Like we said, anyone can become dependent on alcohol. Our theory is that writers get pegged as heavy drinkers because our work puts us in the public eye more often than, say, a chemist's or mid-level salesperson's work, and because we're perceived as reckless thrill-seekers or sensitive, tortured souls susceptible to the idea that alco-hol can loosen our tongues, ergo make the words flow a little easier.

We know dozens of successful writers, some of whom eschew alcohol, and others who really, really love a good cocktail or enjoy making (and drinking) homebrewed beer or wine. However, they don't require a glass of wine or a mixed drink to write. If you're drinking because you crave it, you can't stop drinking once you start, or drinking is starting to impair your relationships—working ones as well as personal ones—then we urge you to talk to your doctor or a trusted friend or family member about your alcohol intake.

In *Macbeth*, Shakespeare said of alcohol, "It provokes the desire, but it takes away the performance." Using alcohol to fuel the creative process is not a good work habit to encourage, even if you have no history of alcoholism. Writing can be emotionally and even physically demanding, but there are better, healthier ways to work through it than with a habitual glass of wine at your keyboard.

BREAK THIS RULE

Stick with magazines; you're a magazine writer, after all.

Many writers, once they've reached writing success, are afraid to step out of the magazine box. However, once you've made it as a magazine writer, you can expand your income by teaching college courses, creating online classes, writing greeting cards, editing textbooks, giving your own seminars, and writing books. You're holding an example of the latter money-maker in your hands right now!

A writer friend of ours and her business partner earned extra money by putting on a writing seminar in Boston. Our friend talked about the business aspect of the job—how to find work—and her partner talked about the actual writing process. They also invited an officer of the National Writers Union to talk about contract issues. The seminar was so successful they decided to do a second one.

Writer Bethanne Kelly Patrick writes "straight-to-the-library" children's nonfiction and curricula. "With shrinking ad pages and magazines closing all over the place," she says, "I believe branching out is the best revenge. Sure, we all like to have 2,000-word features in the glossies, but some of this education writing I do is so enjoyable I can't believe that I get paid as much as I do."

Linda once made a few extra bucks by selling a greeting card idea to a card publisher. Companies also exist that buy your short quips and poetry for mugs, T-shirts, buttons, posters, and more.

You can even do copywriting for magazines. For example, Diana was hired to write cover lines for a revamped trade magazine. The editorial staff was having a difficult time understanding the publisher's directive, so they needed someone who could look at the magazine with a fresh perspective. After a few issues, the magazine took this fun work in-house, but not before paying Diana a hefty consulting fee.

So don't feel you're stuck in the pages of magazines forever if you need to earn more income or if you're burned out dealing with editors and their hoop-jumping. Magazine writing is a wonderful jumping-off point for all kinds of lucrative freelance gigs.

BREAK THIS RULE

You can't do magazine writing and business writing.

We mentioned above that magazine writing can lead to well-paying gigs in other fields, including copywriting, and this is true...but we need to add a caveat here.

As a fledgling freelance writer, Linda thought her pitch for a profile of a young businesswoman would look much more impressive if she mentioned her copywriting credentials. A few weeks later, Linda received a call from the editor. She loved the idea, but because of the copywriting mention she suspected the profile subject might be one of Linda's clients. The thought that Linda's article might really be an advertorial (an ad disguised as an article) caused the editor to reject the idea altogether.

Many magazines you see on the newsstand walk a fine line between journalism and advertising. Consider an article on pet health placed conveniently across from an ad for pet food. Or the piece on easy chicken dinners paired with an ad for prepared frozen chicken. In light of this chummy relationship between editorial and advertising, why would a magazine editor balk at the thought of a freelancer being involved in both of those fields?

"As the saying goes, the appearance of evil is as bad as the evil itself," says Tom Bivins, a professor of media ethics in the School of Journalism and Communication at the University of Oregon. "Even if it's not a real conflict of interest, if people perceive it to be, then it might as well be." In other words: Life ain't fair. The editor's job is to deliver the best possible information to readers, so if an editor thinks you're working in the best interest of your clients instead of the magazine's readership—even if this same editor's magazine overflows with "news" about cosmetics or gas grills—then you've got a problem.

Business writing represents a lucrative opportunity for magazine writers to boost their bottom lines without stepping too far out of their comfort zones. It requires the same level of effort and know-how on the part of the writer. The hard part is ethically balancing copywriting and editorial activities—and convincing editors that your sense of balance is impeccable.

We know you can keep a comfortable gap between church and state, so to speak, but how can you convince editors of this? Follow these tips:

Draw the line.

The best policy is to draw clear boundaries between your business writing and editorial activities. While most editors won't penalize you for being involved in copywriting, they may shun a writer who creates advertising content for companies in the same industry the magazine covers. "If you've written advertorials for face cream, that doesn't matter to us," says Karen Axelton, former executive editor of Entrepreneur.com. "But if you've written advertorials for franchises—well, we do a lot of coverage on franchise opportunities."

Come clean.

If an editor asks you to write about one of your business clients, let the editor know about this conflict of interest. Linda was once approached by a men's fitness magazine to write an article on pre- and post-exercise nutrition, and she let him know she had recently done paid blogging for a protein shake manufacturer. The editor was fine with it, and Linda was able to take the assignment with a clear conscience.

Don't ask, don't tell.

If the editor doesn't ask whether you've done business writing, and in your mind no conflict of interest comes between your advertorial activities and your assignment for this magazine, keep your lip zipped.

In short, don't worry about the "rule" that you can't do editorial writing and business writing. Be careful to keep the two separate and you can earn well from both.

As a freelancer, you've always got to be hustling.

Once editors discover your incredible writing talents, your amazing ability to turn in assignments on time, and the endless depths of your idea well, you'll find yourself spending more time chasing down leads, interviewing sources, and completing paid assignments. What a problem to have, right?

The trouble is that some freelancers find it difficult to slow down. Some even begin to tire of the freelance lifestyle, but they feel compelled to take on more assignments. (This is where Linda raises her hand.) The stories they're working on don't excite them. Because they've been doing well financially, their expenses may be higher than they were during their salad days. There may be a mortgage or a new baby in the picture. That means increased pressure to keep the money flowing in at a fast clip. Soon, the once enthusiastic freelancer turns into a burned-out shell of his former happy self.

We feel that if you're freelancing, you might as well take advantage of one of the major benefits the occupation offers—the ability to do what you want when you want. Yes, marketing yourself is important, but taking care of yourself and not burning out is equally important. People who work for companies other than their own can rarely take a three-hour lunch, bring their kids to a weekday movie matinee, or spend an afternoon kicking back with a good book. But you can...and should!

When Diana started freelancing full time, she continued to schedule hairdressing appointments on Saturdays. That's because if she scheduled them during her lunch hour at her previous job, she spent what was supposed to be a relaxing, pampering time worrying about sneaking into the office without her evil boss noticing she took an extra six minutes for lunch. Then one day, after she'd gone freelance, as she struggled with her hairdresser to find a mutually convenient time on a Saturday, it dawned on her: She was her own boss now. And this new boss gave her permission to get her hair done during the week, those six minutes be damned.

If you feel yourself burning out, make plans now to rest your body, mind, and soul. Take a vacation or a mini-break. Visit an old friend in another state. Take up a new hobby or revisit an old one. Do anything that gets you out of the office. And if you have a hard time convincing yourself that the world won't fall apart if you step away from the desk, we say you *really* need to walk away.

Can't afford a mini-break? Make a rule that you step away from work on the weekends. Several years ago, Diana decided to unplug over the weekends. On Friday evenings, she signs off email, turns her laptop off, and puts her work phone on mute until Monday morning so she can focus on her family and hobbies that rejuvenate and relax her. It has been one of the best mental health decisions she's ever made...and it doesn't cost a dime.

If you look at books, blogs, and websites by many expert writers (or entrepreneurs of any type), it seems like they're always hustling—they're posting on every social media platform non-stop, bragging that they field emails at 2 am, and announcing a new gig they landed every other day— and they recommend you do the same. But we've been in this business for two decades and are here to tell you that rule is *bogus*. Take care of yourself so you can do better work and earn more with less stress.

BREAK THIS RULE

Take advantage of freelance job boards, content sites, and auctions to land more work.

This chapter is about not only surviving, but thriving, so chances are you have some freelance work already but are looking to up your income. As you look around for new gigs, you'll probably run across one of the dozens of freelance project search sites, bidding sites, and so on that have popped up online. These services let you do everything from post your profile to bid on writing projects, and all the other writers you know are in there vying for work. But are they worth it?

Probably not. For one thing, tire-kickers love these sites. Tire-kickers are the junky leads, the prospects who suck your time and knowledge and give you nothing in return. On freelance project boards, anyone can pose as an actual hiring company and request that you do "sample assignments." Enough freelancers do these "sample assignments" and the scammers have their entire project done...for free!

These "buyers" also scan the job boards, gather names, send out a mass email, collect the information they want from freelancers—like hourly rates and quotes on bogus projects—then use the information for purposes other than hiring writers.

Many of the clients who troll these boards are searching for cheap labor, and regrettably the freelancers who participate are only too happy to oblige. Aspiring freelance writers price their goods as if they're Walmart and the other freelancers are competing mom-and-pop operations. For example, one writer on one of these boards worked on eight projects and earned a total of $470, which works out to less than $60 per project. Not exactly enough to pay the rent.

That's not to say sweet gigs can't be found on these sites. Carol Tice of Make a Living Writing coined the term "move-up mills" for sites that are somewhat like content mills, but pay better rates; Skyword and Contently are examples of these.

Don't feel you need to spend any time at all on sites like these; you can get plenty of work the old-fashioned way, and qualify your prospects to boot. But if you want to try posting a profile, bidding on work, or getting in with a content site to boost your income, be sure you're working with reputable sites that pay well and on time.

BREAK THIS RULE

You've got to wear a lot of hats as a freelancer.

When you're starting out, yes, you're pretty much on your own; as they say, you're the chief cook and bottle washer. However, once you've gotten to a certain level of income, you may want to consider hiring help so you can do what you're best at and earn more.

Some examples of help you can hire:

- A virtual assistant to update your website, schedule interviews, handle email, and more.
- A transcriptionist to transcribe your interviews.
- A professional researcher or a local college student to gather research for your assignments.
- An accountant to take care of your taxes.
- A professional organizer to take care of the mess in your office so you can work more productively.
- Coaches and mentors who can help you move up to the next level. (Linda coaches writers, by the way!)
- Billing services to handle your invoicing and collections.
- An interviewer to schedule and conduct interviews while you do the actual writing.

These are only a few examples; get creative and you'll find you can outsource almost any task that's keeping you from focusing on your core competencies. So don't feel that you'll always be working alone and wearing multiple hats; while many writers take the term "freelancer" to strictly mean "solo worker," it's not an absolute rule.

BREAK THIS RULE

Only quitters quit.

You left your 9-to-5 job to freelance full time after saving up a year's worth of income and building up a small stable of clients. Every year your writing income has increased. You've found new clients, developed some additional specialties, and maybe even branched out into book authorship, teaching, or public speaking. Every week there's something new, but free-lancing doesn't seem like such a big deal anymore. People who don't really know you would look at you and say, "Wow, she's made it. She's a real writer!"

But on the inside? On the inside you feel like, "This is *it*?"

It's a struggle because so many people want to be writers that once you've made it, it can feel almost blasphemous to admit you're thinking about doing something else with your life besides writing for clients.

Several years ago, Diana considered going back to school to get a master's degree in nursing. A few of her writing friends were baffled when she announced her plans. She was doing well as a writer, and she was going to walk away from that? How could she? But people who really knew her knew that she'd actually planned on a medical career after college, and only nixed that plan because of a class called organic chemistry. Moreover, she's one of those writers who doesn't find the act of writing all that pleasurable.

Linda, like Diana, has experienced periods of burnout with writing. Occasionally she'll put all her clients on hold to pursue something new, like writing books, teaching classes, or coaching writers. Then she'll feel refreshed and start pitching again. She's probably gone back and forth at least three or four times in the last 20 years.

There's no law that says you have to stick with writing for clients for the rest of your life, even if it *is* a career many people dream about. If financially you can't make ends meet, it's okay to take a break and so something else that pays better or with more regularity. Ditto if you're bored or burned out by the constant hustle of pitching and writing. You are not a failure or a quitter. In fact, you are very smart to realize the limitations you're facing and to do what you feel is best to remedy the problem.

RENEGADE RULE-BREAKER

MJ Plaster

From the moment MJ Plaster transitioned from a tech writer and landed a cover story in *LowCarb Energy* magazine as her first writing gig, she was hooked on freelancing.

Did you break any rules in breaking into this magazine?

Most of them! In the beginning, I didn't know any better. I learned during my tech-writing career to take interesting and challenging jobs even if I didn't have a clue, and I still do that today. If the gig sounds interesting, I'm all in. I didn't even know enough to be afraid to intrude upon the editor's time. I just worked through the query process like I do everything else—like a bull in a china shop!

Before submitting the query, I read a few articles on query letters, and I knew my subject cold. I tried to mimic the structure of the "formula," including a killer lede, some statistics, an anecdote, and an abbreviated outline. Brevity has never been my strong suit when I'm trying to persuade, so I covered all the bases. If a query is a snack, I submitted a cruise ship's midnight buffet.

With zero clips, I wrote the query like I intended to write the article, only longer! I emphasized my former technical writing and instructional design experience. Since it was a low-carb publication, I don't think it hurt that I mentioned I've followed the controlled-carb lifestyle almost since Dr. Atkins published his diet in the 70s.

It was quite a rush to have my very first query accepted and see my first article in print. The thing that I will always remember is the sheer terror when, 48 hours after I submitted the query, the editor gave me the assignment. Everything was academic up to that point.

What challenges did come up against in getting published, and how did you overcome them?

The lack of clips was my biggest challenge. I couldn't include an old help file or software course manual with the query to illustrate my talent.

I wrote for a content mill for a couple of months just to get the clips—and I told no one until now. I inserted the clips at the end of an email rather than including a link. I was very careful to write a few of those keyword articles as if my life depended upon them. I was able to parlay those clips into much better writing jobs, and I included magazine clips the minute I got published. I still look at each job as "this or something better...," "this" being what I currently have on my plate. Over the years, I have dropped less interesting gigs for more interesting gigs. In some cases, "interesting" means "better paying."

Why did you decide to get into writing?

I was educated by Dominican nuns. They have a profound effect on your sense of what's important, and writing was always at the top of their list. My mother was a magazine editor, and that had some influence. The third and final straw was moving to New York and flying to Europe once a week at the ripe old age of 21. I've been writing since my flight attendant days, because I wanted to capture the memories. My first gig was a newspaper travel column. In the late 80s, I accidentally fell into technical writing, instructional design, and consulting while taking leaves from the airline. When outsourcing tossed me off of that merry-go-round, a close high school friend suggested that I should be writing for magazines. She was right—for a time, but that's no longer my focus.

Do you have any advice for new writers looking to break into magazines?

Yes, I've learned five major lessons:

1. **Do it your way** (as validated in *The Renegade Writer*, by the way). It's important to come across in your writing as genuine. It is possible to maintain a professional demeanor while letting the world see that you have a persona to go along with your brains. I have a couple of clients who ask me to pull from my experiences in each article.

2. **When you start writing, keep quiet about it.** Most people around you will do everything in their power to dissuade you. When you find others of like mind, stick to them like glue. Encourage them when they need it, and they'll provide a kick in the pants when you need it.

3. **You don't have to learn everything at once.** It's easier to master each little slice of the pie on a need-to-know basis, a little at a time. It scares me how little I still know, but I'm too busy to dwell on it.

4. **Submit queries or letters of introduction to new opportunities the minute you learn about them, before the window of opportunity closes.** When you get the assignment, deliver more than you promised.

5. **Get over print.** There are plenty of lucrative online opportunities, and they're easier to land.

It's been ten years since you spoke to us. How has your career changed?

I accidentally fell into magazine editing a decade ago. A friend who is a publisher asked me to come on board "to save an account." Once again, I didn't have the first clue! Five magazines later with various publishers, I have returned to my first magazine, working directly with the association as their editor-in-chief. Other than the editing gig, I have switched to online writing—eight newsletters a month for a property management company, with the rest of the month devoted to writing for operations ranging from Fortune 500 companies to mom-and-pop businesses. I would have to be offered some very serious money to drop any of my current clients.

New writers need to stretch beyond their current skillset and think big. Develop a winning attitude. How can you make it big by thinking small? There's a whole range of jobs between content mills and national consumer magazines. Don't marry yourself to an outcome, and the perfect job will find you—but you have to do the work to receive the job offers, and you have to deliver once you get the gig.

About the Authors

Linda Formichelli has written for over 150 magazines, from *Pizza Today* to *Woman's Day*; authored and co-authored over a dozen books, including *Commit: How to Blast Through Problems & Reach Your Goals Through Massive Action*; and guest posted at top blogs like Copyblogger, Tiny Buddha, and Write to Done.

Diana Burrell is a Boston-based food writer, recipe developer, and author who has written for *Parenting*, *Cook's Illustrated*, *The Boston Globe*, *Kiwi*, *Family Circle*, *Psychology Today*, *Writer's Digest*, and many other national, regional, and closed-circulation publications.

Like This Book?
Here Are More Like It
(Plus Your Free Gift!)

Thank you for purchasing and reading *The Renegade Writer*...and now we'd like to send you a free gift. Here's where you can get a free copy of *The Renegade Writer OMNIBUS: Best of the Renegade Writer Blog 2006-2016*, a compilation of over 900 posts from the award-winning (and now defunct) Renegade Writer Blog!

BookHip.com/SJRVJP

If you enjoyed reading *The Renegade Writer*, we would love to read your review on Amazon.com, Goodreads, your own blog, or anywhere else! Reviews help build readership, which will help support our efforts at delivering more renegade writing advice for writers through Renegade Writer Press.

Other Books By Renegade Writer Press:

- *The Renegade Writer's Query Letters That Rock* by Linda Formichelli and Diana Burrell
- *The Renegade Writer OMNIBUS: Best of the Renegade Writer Blog 2006-2016* by Linda Formichelli and Diana Burrell
- *Rock-Solid Queries: The 10 Surprising Reasons Why Magazine Editors Reject Your Ideas...and How to Write Queries That Get More Acceptances Today* by Diana Burrell
- *Write Your Way Out of the Rat Race...and Step Into a Career You Love* by Linda Formichelli
- *Become a Confident Freelance Writer* by Linda Formichelli and Diana Burrell

We have lots, lots more for writers like you at the Renegade Writer Press website:

www.renegadewriterpress.com

Acknowledgments

We'd like to thank the many editors, experts, and freelance writers who generously shared their expertise with us in the first, second, and now third editions of *The Renegade Writer*: Matthew Alderton, Carol Alexander, Brian Alm, Moira Allen, Judy Artunian, Ed Avis, Karen Axelton, Karen Dove Barr, Dick Baumer, Lisa Beamer, Monica Bhide, Tom Bivens, Greg Blanchette, Maggie Bonham, Cynthia Boris, Elisa Bosley, Damon Brown, Mary-Beth Bruno, Simone Carter, Iyna Boyt Caruso, Sheilagh Casey, Monique Cuvelier, Doug Delp, Rachel Dickinson, Maureen Dixon, Howard Faulkner, Dan Ferber, Denise Foley, Brett Forrest, Kathleen Furore, Jenna Glatzer, Craig Grigson III, Lisa Hannam, Brett Harvey, Evan Harvey, Renee Heiss, Don Hinkle, Arnold Howard, Kelly James, Daniel Kehrer, Mary Kennedy, Dian Killian, Angela Giles Klocke, Jennifer Lawler, Nancy LePatourel, Kim Lisi, Linda Moran, Roxanne Nelson, Bob Neubauer, Melanie Nicsinger, Liz Palmer, Bethanne Kelly Patrick, Leslie Pepper, Kaja Perina, Jennie Phipps, MJ Plaster, Rebecca Rolfes, Chip Rose, Anne M. Russell, Jenna Schnuer, Beth Lee Segal, Jane Simons/Felicity West, Elissa Sonnenberg, John Stark, Alison Stein, Roy Stevenson, Julie Sturgeon, Wendy Lyons Sunshine, Cindy Sweeney, Mary Beth Temple, James D. Thwaites, Carol Tice, Lynne Ticknor, Don Vaughan, Melody Warnick, Judy Waytiuk, Jennifer Weeks, Jeremy White, and Arline Zatz.

We appreciate and value the professionals who helped us redesign and layout this third edition of *The Renegade Writer*, Maria at BEAUTeBOOK and Jason at Polgarus Studio.

We are eternally grateful to the thousands of you who followed our blog, bought our books, or took classes from us. Your support through the years means so much to us.

We would both like to thank our families, who have done everything from proofreading and making copies, to babysitting and listening to our kvetching. We love you!